D U B L I N

STREET & ATLAS GUIDE

CONTENTS

Scale of maps is 1:15,000 (4.2 inches to 1 mile)

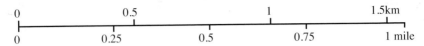

LEGEND

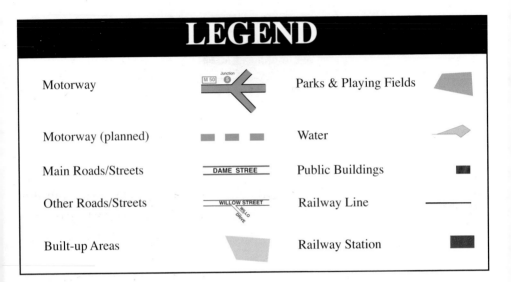

Motorway		Parks & Playing Fields
Motorway (planned)		Water
Main Roads/Streets	DAME STREE	Public Buildings
Other Roads/Streets	WILLOW STREET	Railway Line
Built-up Areas		Railway Station

© Causeway Press (N.I.) 1999

The maps on pages 4 to 41 are based upon the Ordnance Survey by permission of the Government of the Republic of Ireland.

Printed by The Universities Press (Belfast) Ltd.

Edited by Paul Slevin. Comments, suggestions and inquiries should be addressed to him at the address below. Published by Causeway Press (N.I.), Enterprise House, Balloo Avenue, Bangor, N.Ireland BT19 7QT. Phone (01247) 271 525. Fax (01247) 270 080.
E-mail causewaypress@eudoramail.com

DISTRIBUTION: Distributed by Eason Wholesale Books (phone Dublin 862 2111) and Argosy Libraries Ltd (phone Dublin 855 2727). Quote ISBN 1 872600 43 3.

ACKNOWLEDGEMENTS: Special thanks go to Catherine Coyle for her help and endurance.

D U B L I N

STREET
ATLAS
GUIDE

W e all like to kill two birds with one stone, so to speak, but the Dublin Street Atlas & Guide is that extremely rare bird which offers several different products for the price of one.

Firstly, it is a street atlas of the greater Dublin area, based on the latest Ordnance Survey. These maps, together with separate rail and bus maps, will help you to navigate your way through and around the city.

Secondly, it is a detailed guide to the best of what Dublin has to offer. Whether you are visiting for the first time or have lived here all your life, our aim is to help you make the most of this vibrant and colourful city.

The guide is written and published in Ireland, and is based on contributions from people who have immersed themselves in the Dublin social scene with scant regard to their need of sleep and the health of their livers. Having said that, we are always keen to hear alternative views. If you have any recommendations to make or any contrary views to express regarding any of our choices, please write, fax or e-mail to the addresses given on the page opposite. Any contributions which we use in the future will be acknowledged and a copy of the next edition will be sent in return for the best letters.

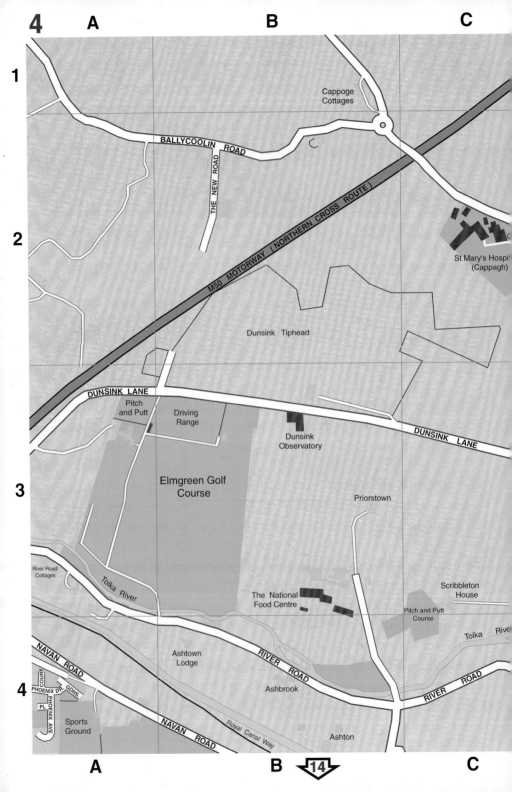

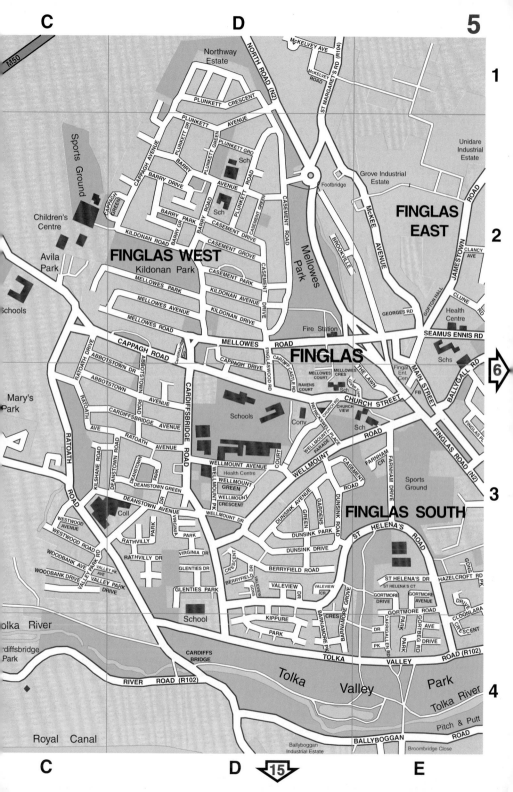

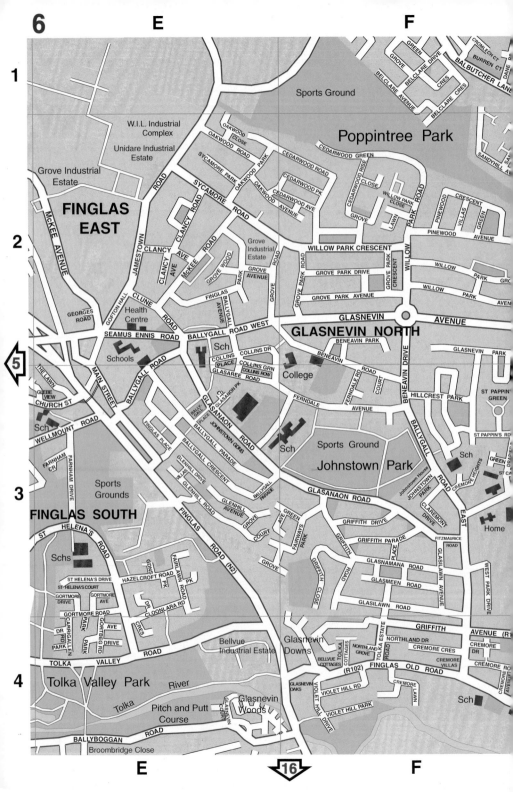

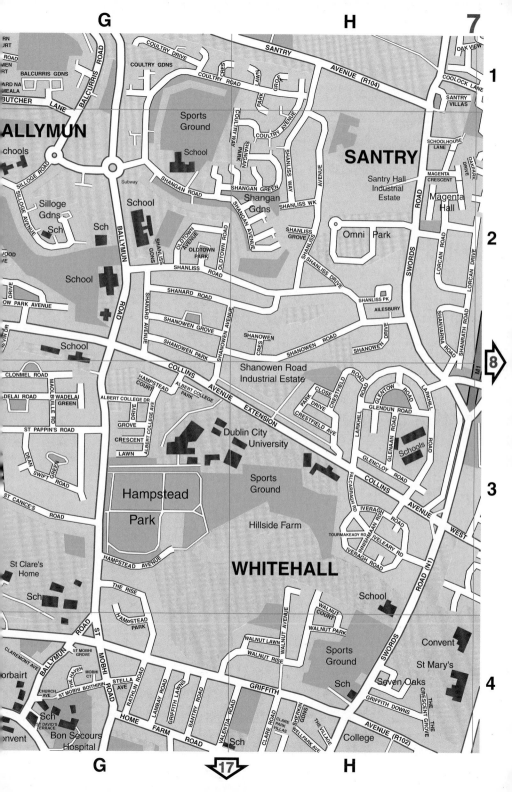

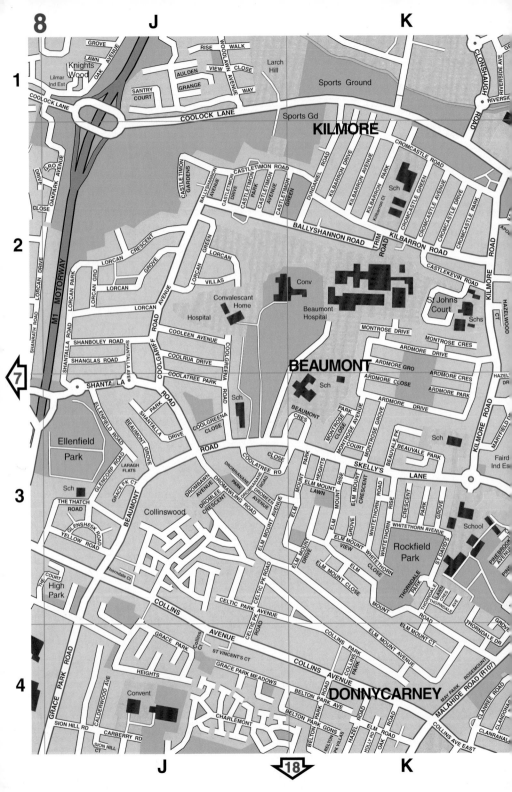

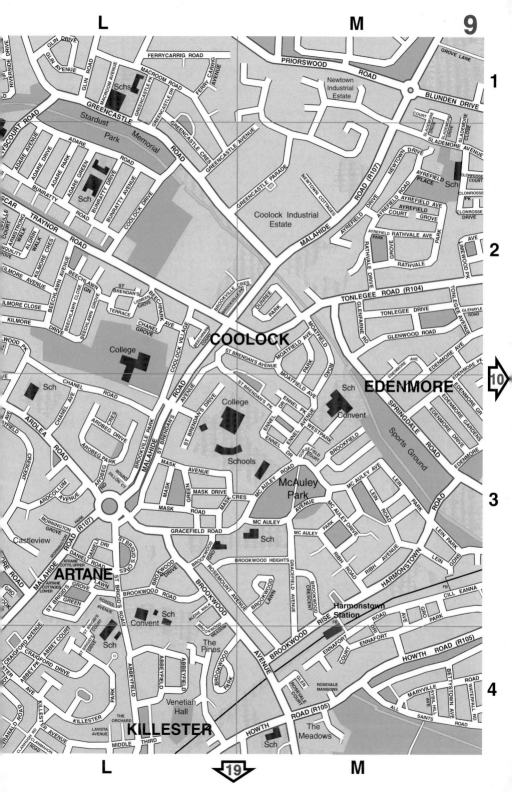

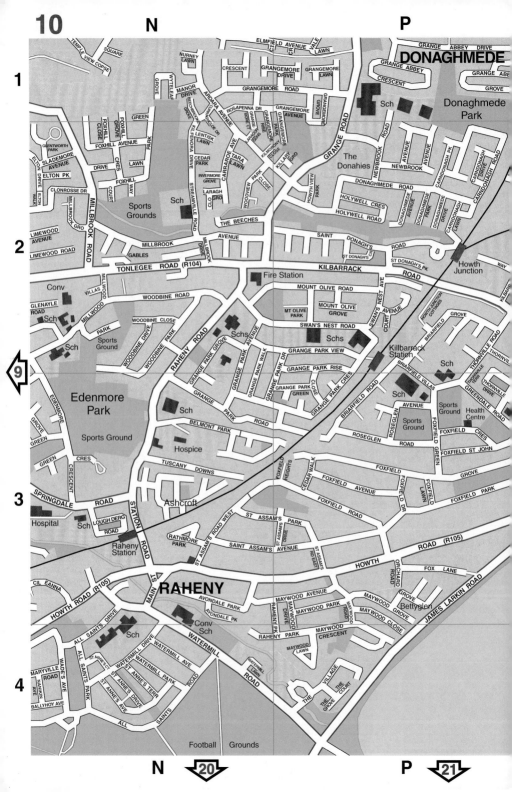

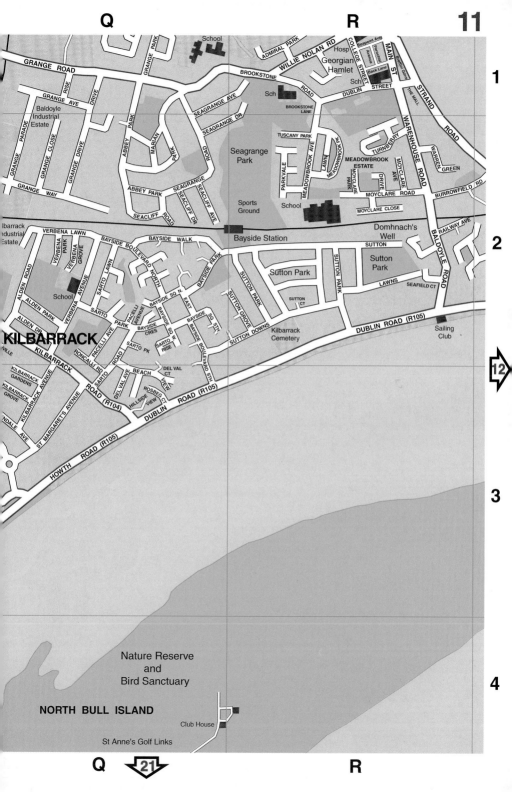

School

GRANGE ROAD

ADMIRAL PARK

WILLIE NOLAN RD

COLLEGE STREET

Seapoint Ave

Hosp

Georgian Hamlet

MAIN ST

Principal Ave

Back Lane

BROOKSTONE ROAD

Sch

STREET

DUBLIN

THE MALL

STRAND ROAD

GRANGE RISE

GRANGE AVE

DRIVE

SEAGRANGE AVE

Sch

BROOKSTONE LANE

Baldoyle Industrial Estate

GRANGE PARADE

GRANGE CLOSE

GRANGE DRIVE

ABBEY PARK

MARIAN PARK

SEAGRANGE DR

SEAGRANGE ROAD

TUSCANY PARK

Seagrange Park

MEADOWBROOK AVE

PARKVALE

LAWN

MEADOWBROOK ESTATE

MEADOWBROOK PK

WARENHOUSE ROAD

TURNBERRY

WARREN GREEN

MOYCLARE AVE

MOYCLARE DRIVE

BURROWFIELD RD

GRANGE WAY

ABBEY PARK

SEAGRANGE

SEACLIFF AVE

SEACLIFF DR

Sports Ground

School

MOYCLARE PARK

MOYCLARE ROAD

MOYCLARE CLOSE

SEACLIFF ROAD

1

lbarrack ndustrial Estate

VERBENA LAWN

BAYSIDE WALK

BAYSIDE BOULEVARD NORTH

Bayside Station

Domhnach's Well

SUTTON

RAILWAY AVE

BALDOYLE ROAD

2

ALDEN ROAD

VERBENA PARK

VERBENA GROVE

VERBENA AVENUE

BAYSIDE PARK

Sutton Park

SUTTON PARK

Sutton Park

LAWNS

SEAFIELD CT

School

SARTO LAWN

SARTO PARK

PACELLI AVENUE

BAYSIDE SQ. N.

BAYSIDE SQ. EAST

SUTTON PARK

SUTTON GROVE

SUTTON CT

ALDEN PARK

ALDEN DR

KILBARRACK

KILBARRACK

PACELLI AVE

BAYSIDE CRES

BAYSIDE SQ W. RISE

BAYSIDE SQ STH

BAYSIDE

SUTTON DOWNS

Kilbarrack Cemetery

DUBLIN ROAD (R105)

Sailing Club

NVILLE

RONCALLI RD

SARTO ROAD

SARTO PK

BEACH VIEW

DEL VAL CT

BAYSIDE BOULEVARD STH

KILBARRACK GARDENS

KILBARRACK AVENUE

SARTO

DEL VAL AVE

HILLSIDE

ROSBEG VIEW

DUBLIN ROAD (R105)

KILBARRACK GROVE

ST MARGARET'S AVENUE

ROAD (R104)

DUBLIN

3

NDALE AVE

HOWTH ROAD (R105)

Nature Reserve and Bird Sanctuary

NORTH BULL ISLAND

Club House

St Anne's Golf Links

4

12

21

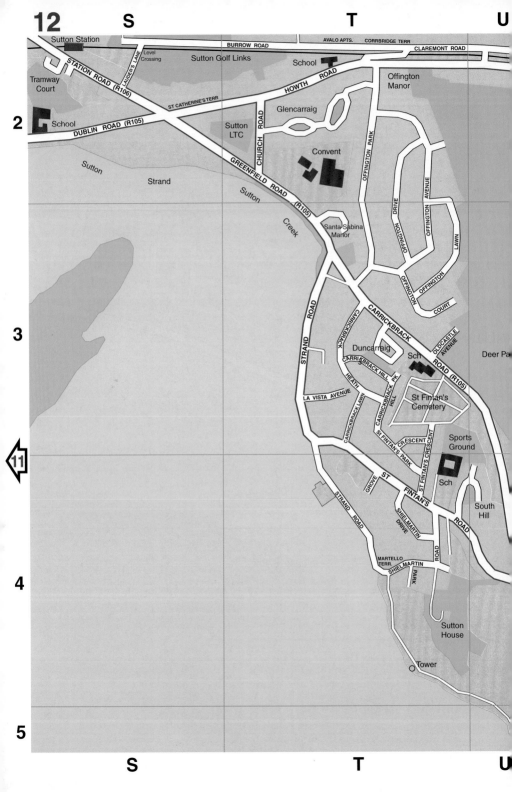

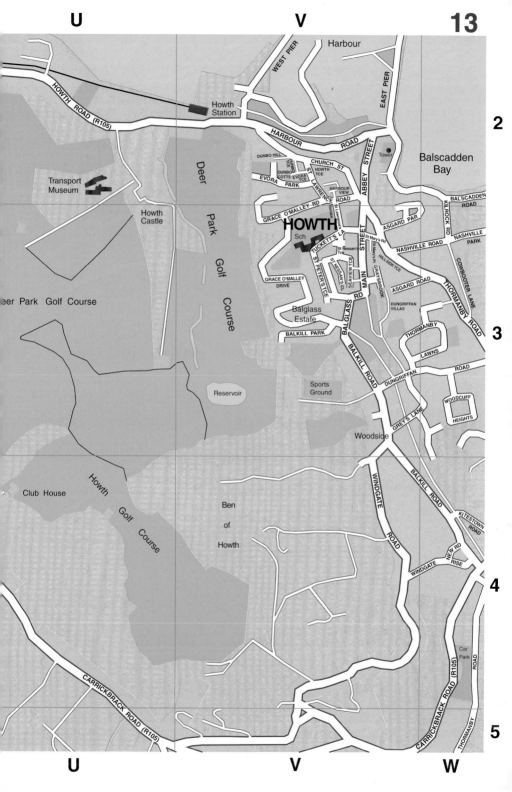

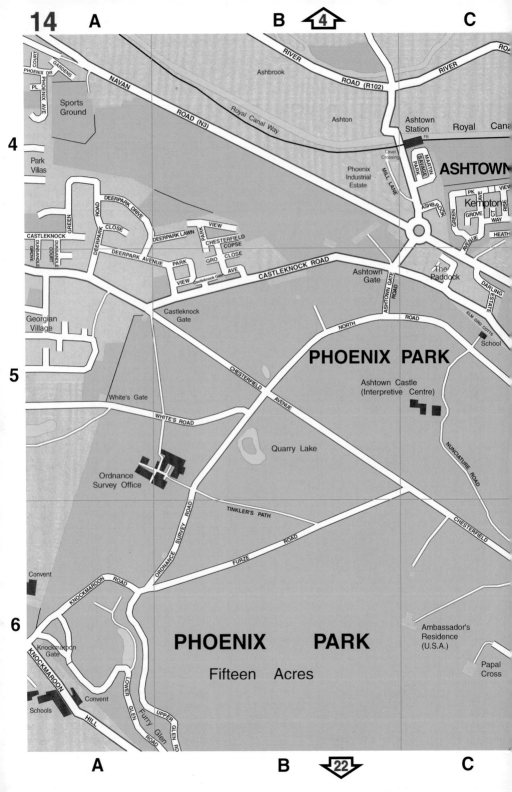

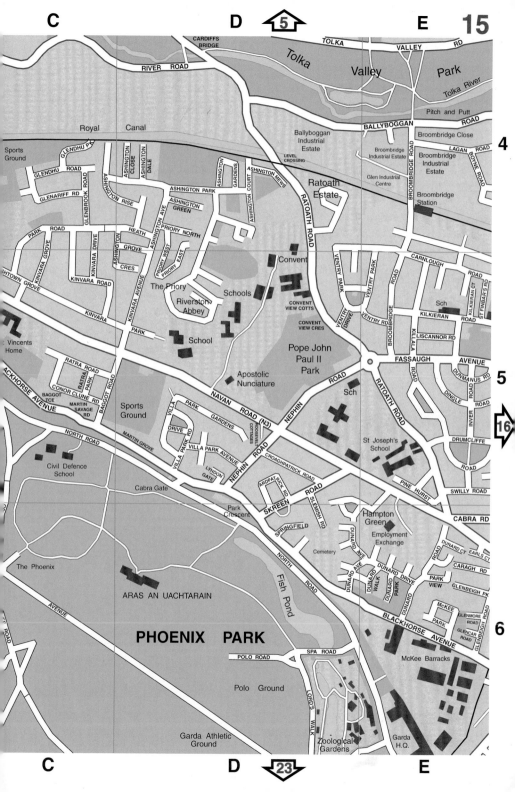

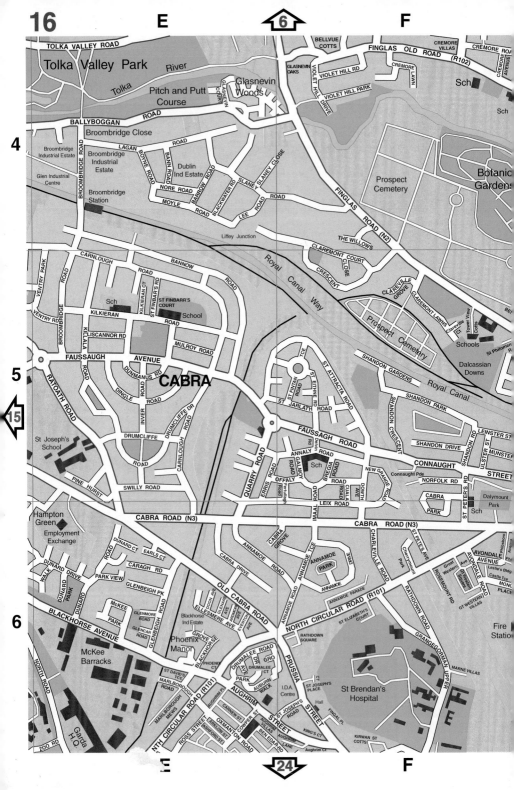

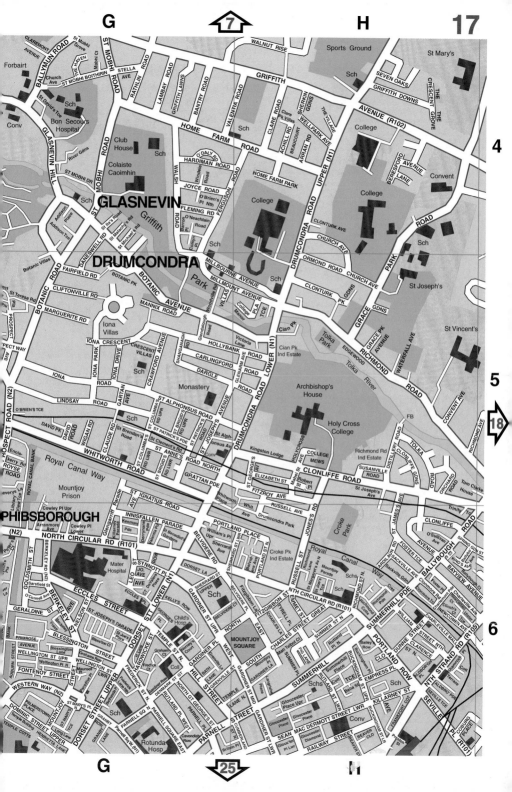

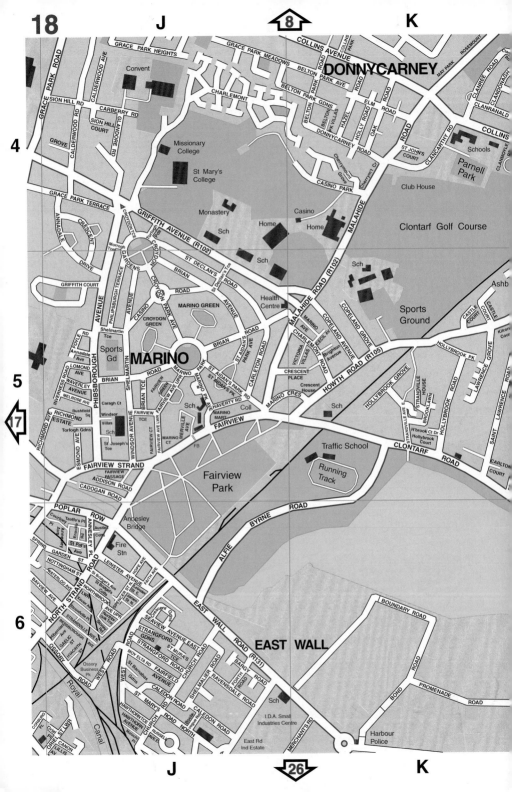

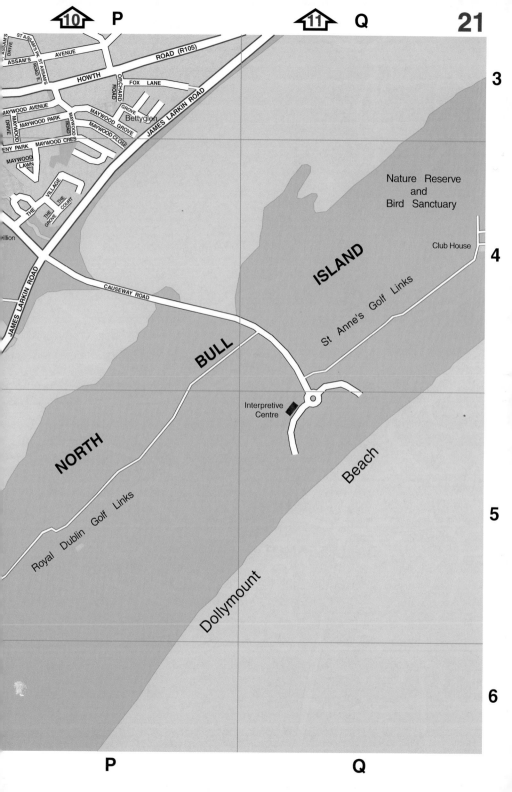

3

ST ASSAM'S DRIVE
ST ASSAM'S PK.
ASSAM'S AVENUE
ASSAM'S
ROAD E.
ST ASSAM'S ROAD
ROAD (R105)
HOWTH
ORCHARD ROAD
FOX LANE
GROVE
MAYWOOD AVENUE
MAYWOOD GROVE
Bettyglen
DRIVE
MAYWOOD PARK
MAYWOOD ROAD
MAYWOOD CLOSE
JAMES LARKIN ROAD
MAYWOOD DRIVE
ENY PARK
MAYWOOD CRES.
MAYWOOD
LAWN

Nature Reserve
and
Bird Sanctuary

THE VILLAGE
THE GROVE
THE COURT

villion

JAMES LARKIN ROAD

Club House

ISLAND

4

CAUSEWAY ROAD

St Anne's Golf Links

BULL

Interpretive
Centre

NORTH

Beach

Royal Dublin Golf Links

5

Dollymount

6

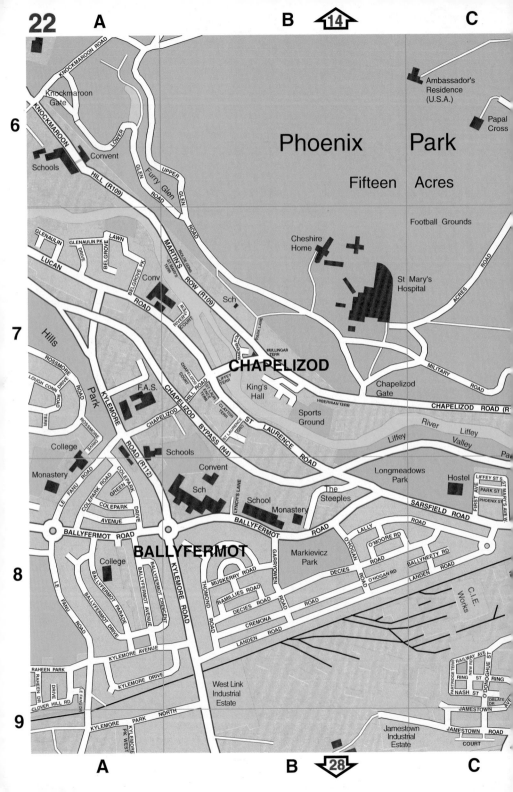

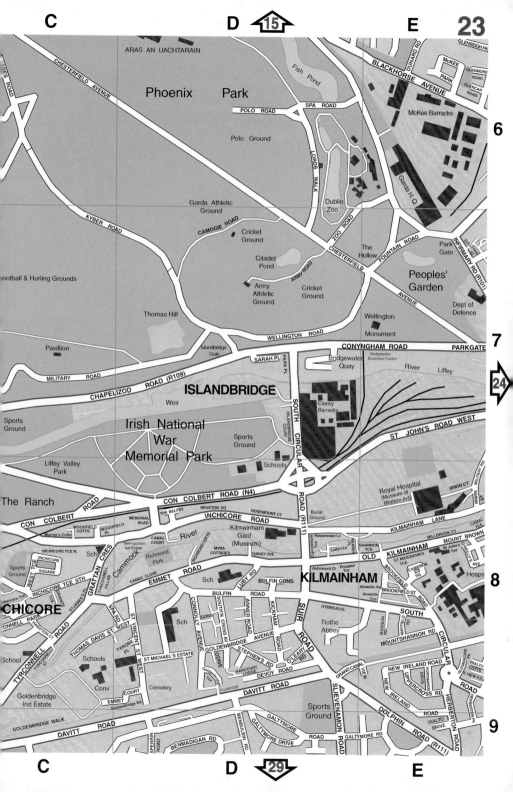

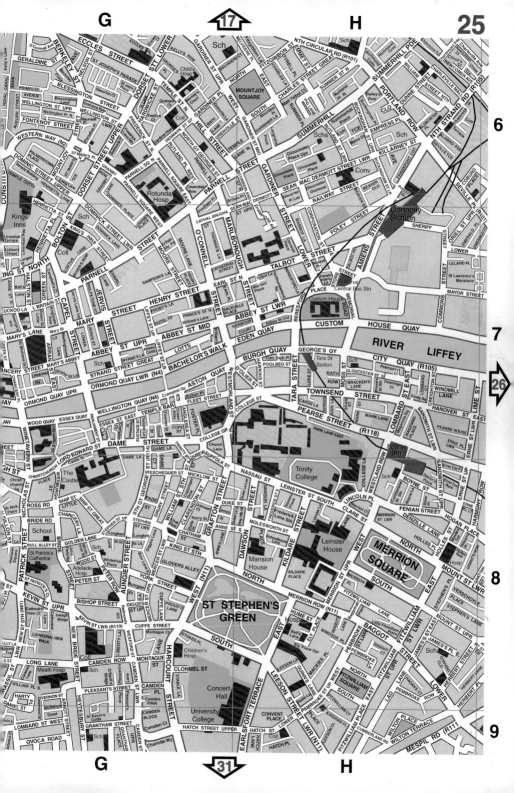

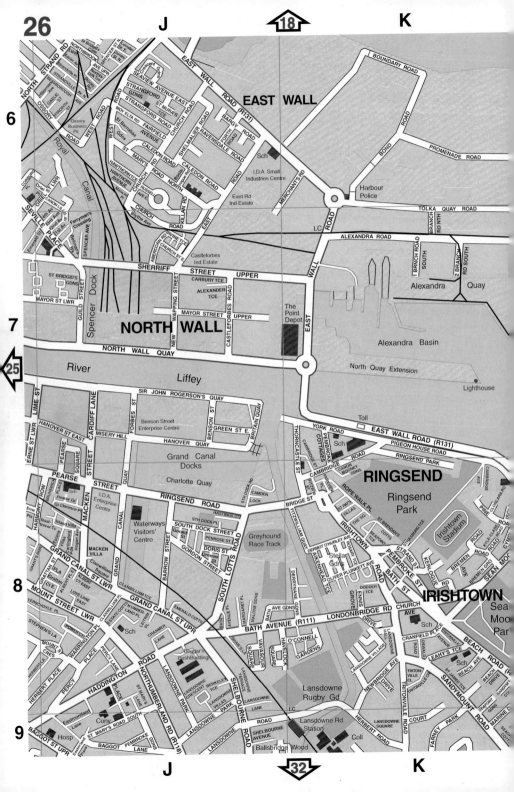

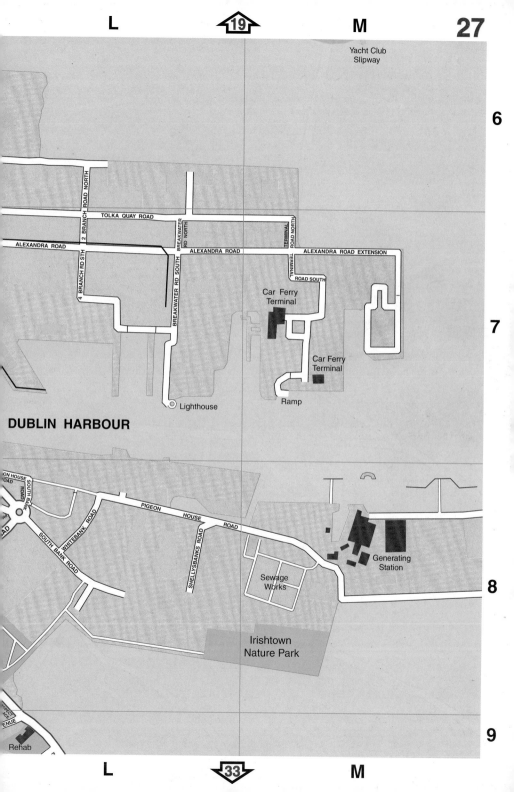

6

Yacht Club
Slipway

2 BRANCH ROAD NORTH

TOLKA QUAY ROAD

BREAKWATER RD NORTH

TERMINAL ROAD NORTH

ALEXANDRA ROAD

4 BRANCH RD STH

ALEXANDRA ROAD

ALEXANDRA ROAD EXTENSION

BREAKWATER RD SOUTH

TERMINAL ROAD SOUTH

7

Car Ferry
Terminal

Car Ferry
Terminal

Lighthouse

Ramp

DUBLIN HARBOUR

ON HOUSE ROAD

SOUTH BANK ROAD

PIGEON HOUSE ROAD

SOUTH BANK ROAD

WHITEBANK ROAD

SHELLYSBANKS ROAD

Generating
Station

8

Sewage
Works

Irishtown
Nature Park

9

Rehab

ENUE

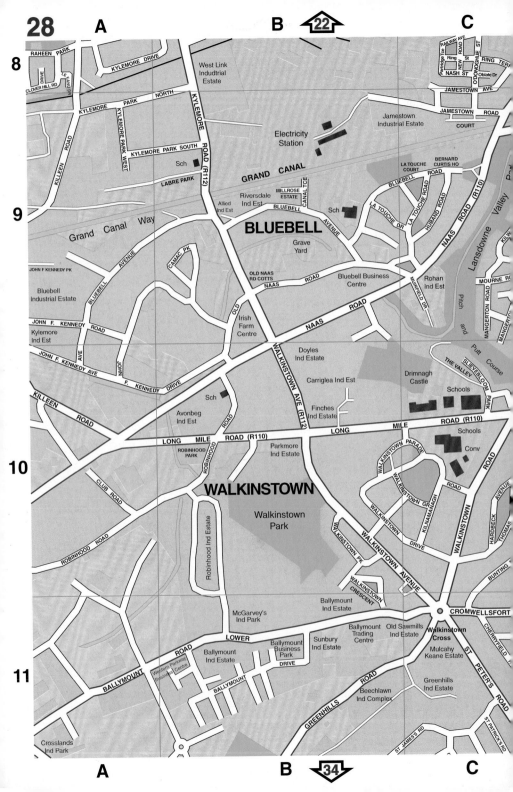

A   B   C

8

RAHEEN PARK

CLOVER HILL RD

KYLEMORE DRIVE

West Link Industrial Estate

KYLEMORE PARK NORTH

KILLEEN ROAD

KYLEMORE PARK WEST

KYLEMORE PARK SOUTH

Sch

LABRE PARK

RIVERSDALE ESTATE

Millrose Ind Est

Allied Ind Est

Electricity Station

Jamestown Industrial Estate

RAILWAY AVE
Partridge Tce   Ring   NEW   St
NASH ST   ROAD   O'DONOGHUE ST
ROW   Oblate Dr

JAMESTOWN AVE

JAMESTOWN ROAD

COURT

LA TOUCHE COURT

BERNARD CURTIS HO

BLUEBELL ROAD

LA TOUCHE ROAD

RUBAND ROAD

9

GRAND CANAL

Grand Canal Way

JOHN F KENNEDY PK

Bluebell Industrial Estate

JOHN F. KENNEDY ROAD

Kylemore Ind Est

JOHN F. KENNEDY AVE

JOHN F. KENNEDY DRIVE

CAMAC PK

BLUEBELL AVENUE

OLD NAAS RD COTTS

NAAS ROAD

OLD NAAS ROAD

Irish Farm Centre

BLUEBELL

Grave Yard

Bluebell Business Centre

CANAL TCE

BLUEBELL AVENUE

Sch

LA TOUCHE DR

NAAS ROAD (R110)

Lansdowne Valley

MOURNE RD

MANGERTON ROAD

Rohan Ind Est

MURFIELD DR

Pitch and

Putt Course

THE VALLEY

SLIEVEBLOOM PARK

KILW

10

KILLEEN ROAD

CLUB ROAD

ROBINHOOD ROAD

Sch

Avonbeg Ind Est

WALKINSTOWN AVE (R112)

Doyles Ind Estate

Carriglea Ind Est

Finches Ind Estate

Drimnagh Castle

Schools

LONG MILE ROAD (R110)

ROBINHOOD PARK

WALKINSTOWN

Parkmore Ind Estate

Walkinstown Park

LONG MILE ROAD (R110)

Schools

Conv

WALKINSTOWN PARADE

WALKINSTOWN GRGH

KILNAMANAGH ROAD

WALKINSTOWN DRIVE

WALKINSTOWN ROAD

HARDBECK AVENUE

BUNTING

THOMAS

11

Robinhood Ind Estate

McGarvey's Ind Park

LOWER BALLYMOUNT ROAD

Ballymount Ind Estate

Western Parkway Business Centre

BALLYMOUNT ROAD

Ballymount Business Park

DRIVE

BALLYMOUNT

Sunbury Ind Estate

Ballymount Ind Estate

Ballymount Trading Centre

Old Sawmills Ind Est

WALKINSTOWN PK

WALKINSTOWN CRESCENT

WALKINSTOWN AVENUE

Walkinstown Cross

CROMWELLSFORT

Mulcahy Keane Estate

GREENHILLS ROAD

Beechlawn Ind Complex

Greenhills Ind Estate

ST PETERS ROAD

CHERYFIELD

Crosslands Ind Park

ST. JAMES'S RD

ST PATRICK'S RD

A   B   C

22

34

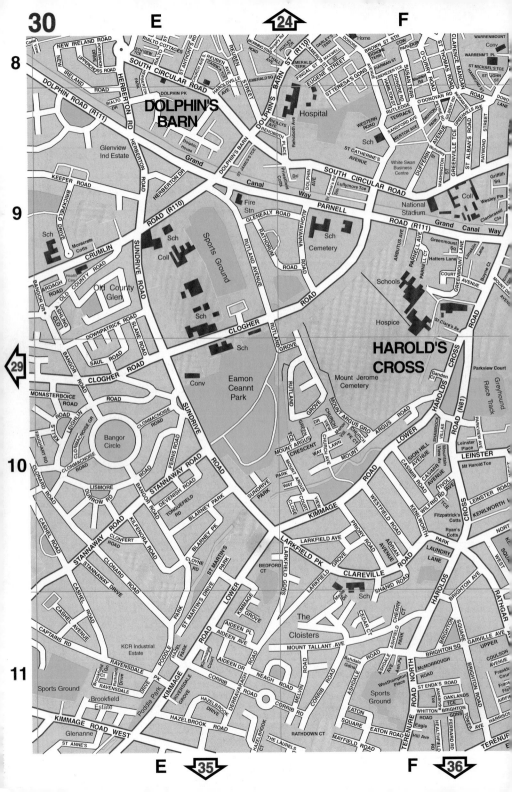

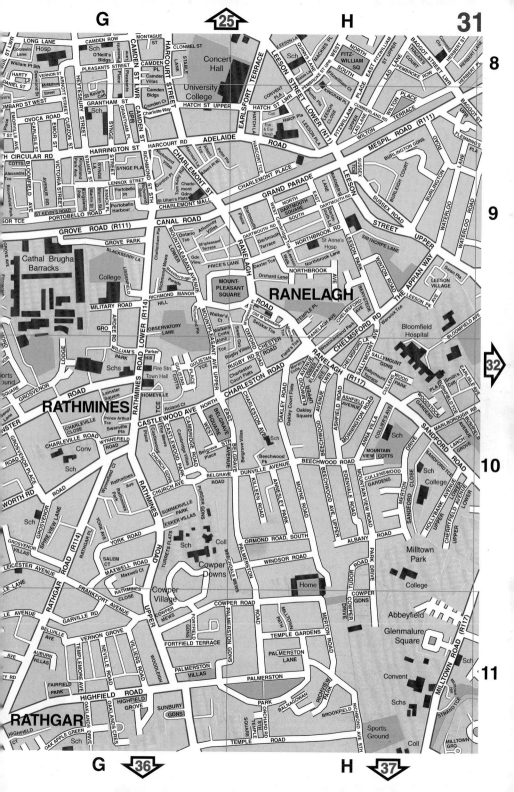

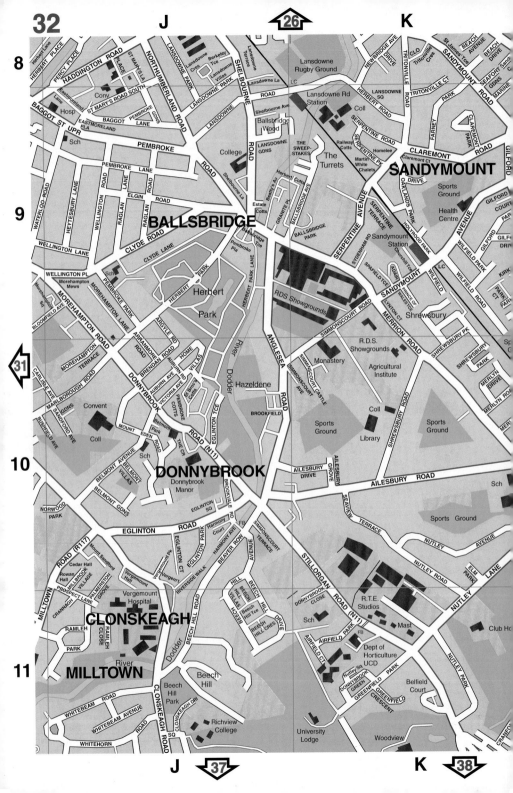

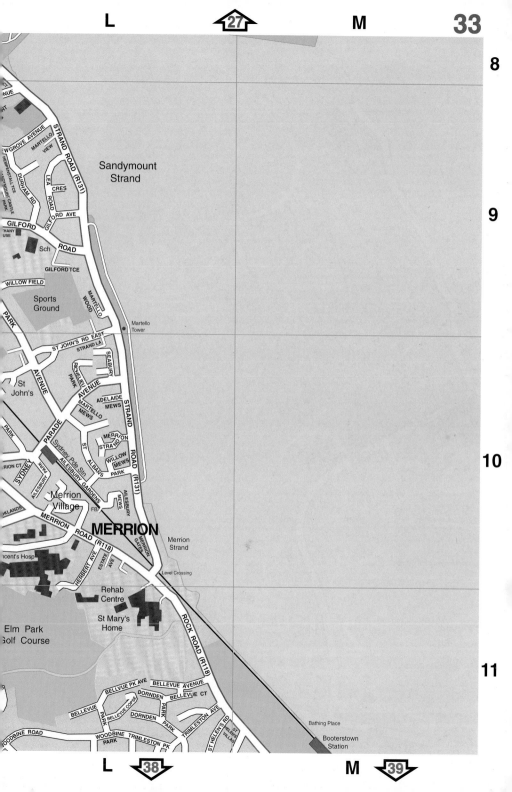

Sandymount
Strand

NUE

RT

EWGROVE AVENUE

MARTELLO
VIEW

STRAND ROAD (R131)

HEBRON STALL TCE

SANDYMOUNT CASTLE
PARK

DURHAM RD

LEA
ROAD

CRES

GILFORD RD AVE

GILFORD

'HANY
USE

Sch

ROAD

GILFORD TCE

WILLOW FIELD

PARK

Sports
Ground

MARTELLO
WOOD

MARTELLO

Martello
Tower

ST JOHN'S RD EAST

STRAND LA

SEABURY

St
John's

AVENUE

RICHELIEU
PARK

AVENUE

ADELAIDE
MEWS

MARTELLO
MEWS

STRAND ROAD (R131)

PARK

PARADE

ST ALBAN'S

MERRION
STRAND

WILLOW
MEWS
PARK

SYDNEY

Sydney Pde Stn

ALLESBURY GARDENS

ALLESBURY
PARK

RION CT

AILESBURY
MEWS

AILESBURY

Merrion
Village

OKLANDS

FB

MERRION

ROAD (R118)

MERRION
GATES

Merrion
Strand

ncent's Hosp

HERBERT AVE

ESTATE
AVE

Level Crossing

Elm Park
Golf Course

Rehab
Centre

St Mary's
Home

ROCK

ROAD (R118)

BELLVUE PK AVE

BELLEVUE AVENUE

DORNDEN

BELLEVUE CT

BELLEVUE
PARK

BELLEVUE COPSE

DORNDEN

PARK

TRIMLESTON AVE

WOODBINE ROAD

WOODBINE
PARK

TRIMLESTON PK

DORNDEN
PARK

ST HELEN'S RD

Bathing Place

Booterstown
Station

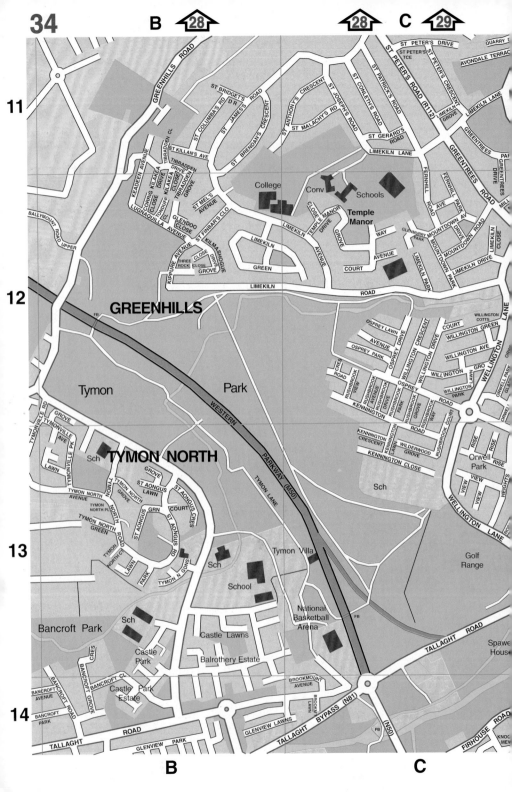

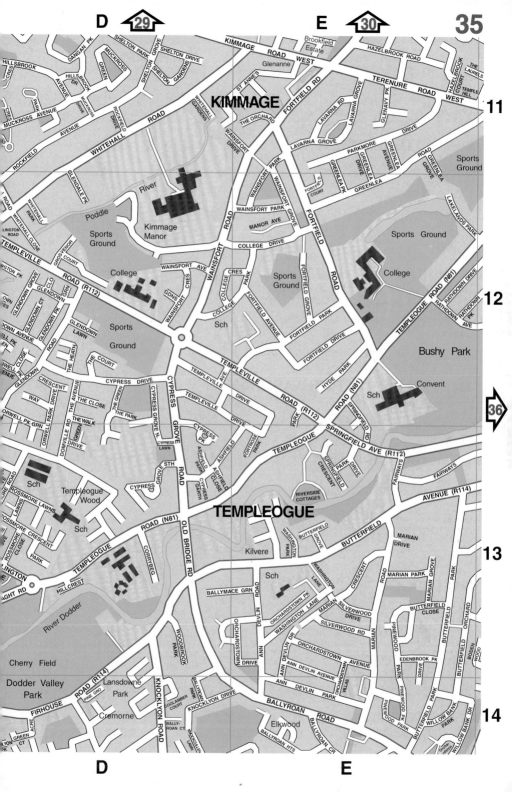

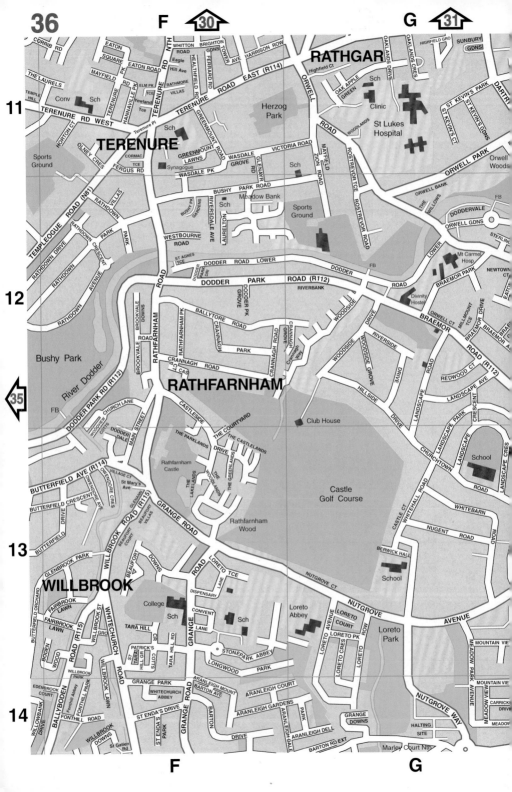

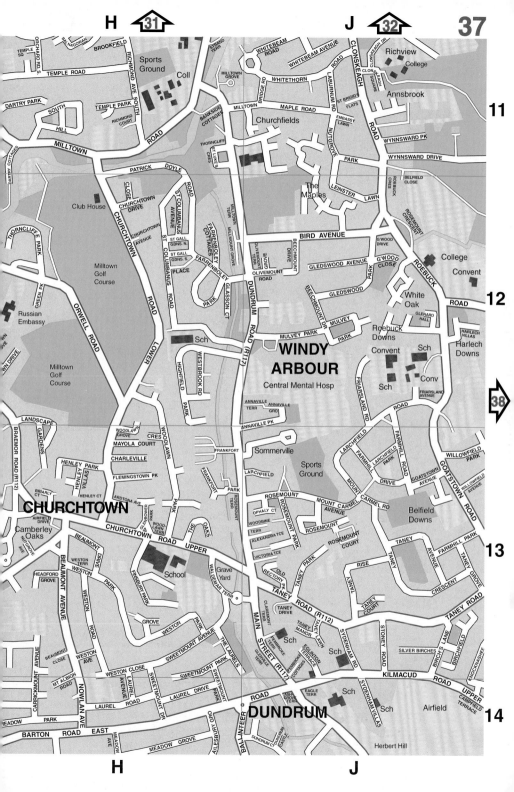

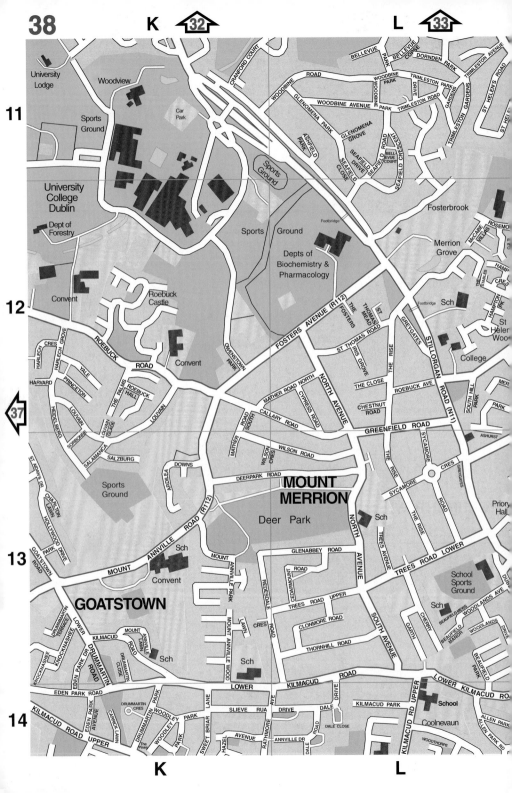

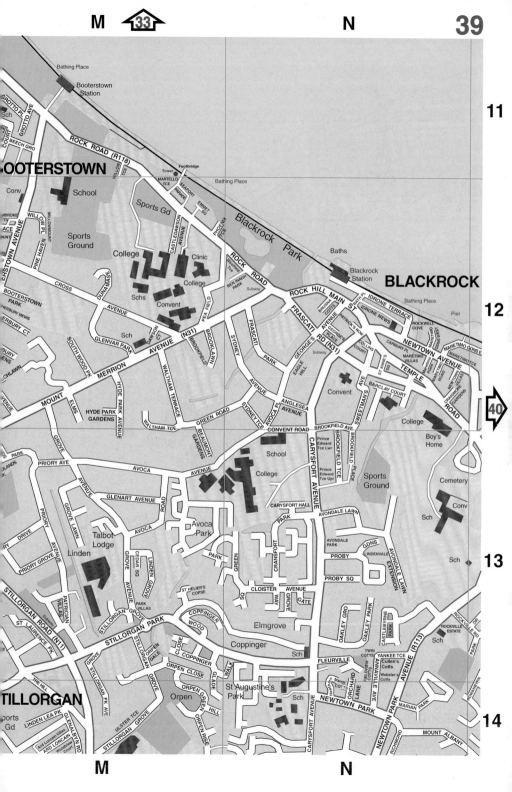

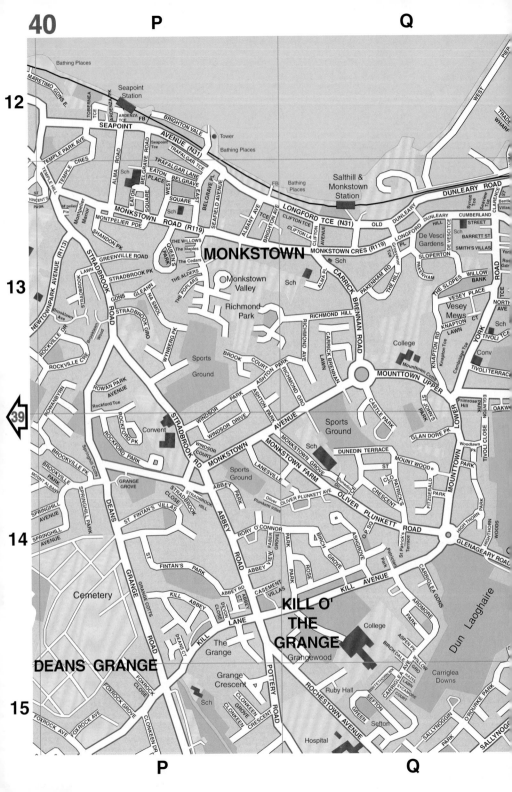

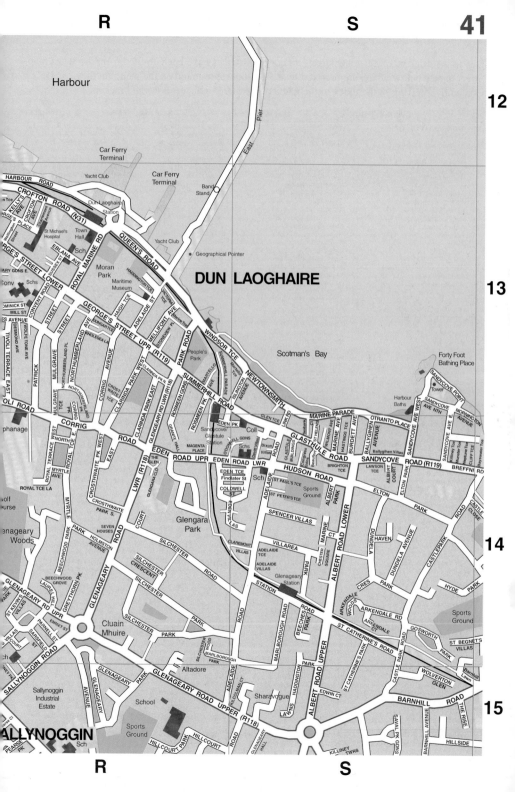

Due to insufficient space, some streets and/or their names have been omitted from the street map. Street names below which are prefixed by a * are not represented on the map, but they can be located by referring in the index to the name of the street which follows in brackets.

STREET INDEX

STREET INDEX

STREET INDEX

STREET INDEX

STREET INDEX

Dublin gets its name from the Gaelic, *dubh linn*, which means dark pool, a reference to the spot where the River Liffey meets the River Poddle, and the first settlement near to this spot dates back more than 5,000 years. Christianity arrived with Saint Patrick in 432 AD, and a golden age of Gaelic Christianity followed which produced such magnificent works of religious art as the Book of Kells which can still be seen today in Trinity College.

The native population remained largely undisturbed by further foreign visitors until the Vikings arrived early in the 9th century. Despite fierce resistance from the native Irish, the Vikings consolidated their presence with victory in the Battle of Dublin in 919 and the town subsequently became an important trading post in the Viking empire.

The Vikings were finally overcome by the Gaelic clans at the Battle of Clontarf in 1014 but their influence is still marked today by place names such as Howth, from the Norse word *hovud* meaning headland, and Leixlip, from the Norse word *laxlep* meaning salmon leap.

The next invaders were Anglo Normans sent by King Henry II. Led by the Earl of Pembroke, who was better known as Strongbow, they landed in Wexford in 1169. Dublin was soon overwhelmed by the strength of their forces and the Normans quickly set about changing the face of Dublin. Henry granted the town a charter in 1171 and established a court there. The oldest surviving buildings in the city date from this period, including Christ Church and Saint Patrick's cathedrals, and parts of Dublin Castle. Due to the fact that wood was the main component of their construction, however, there is very little of the original buildings left for us to see today.

English customs and the English language prevailed in and around the city, within an area which became known as the Pale, but the Irish chieftains held sway elsewhere, giving rise to the phrase 'beyond the Pale'. By 1542, Henry VIII had proclaimed himself King of Ireland as well as England, and the Reformation came to Ireland. Dublin became Protestant, and grew in importance as royal authority spread to other parts of Ireland. By 1592 the College of the Holy and Undivided Trinity of Queen Elizabeth was founded on land confiscated from the Priory of All Hallows. Commonly known as Trinity College, this Protestant seat of learning has played an illustrious role in Dublin's history over the past 400 years.

With Charles I beheaded and the English monarchy abolished, Oliver Cromwell landed in Dublin with a large army in 1649, ushering in a particularly bloody and savage era in Irish history. After the restoration of the monarchy in 1660, Dublin began to take on much of the shape which we recognise today. St Stephen's Green and the Phoenix Park were laid out and many significant public buildings were erected including the Royal Hospital in Kilmainham, now the Museum of Modern Art.

By 1685 the Catholic King James II was on the throne and Ireland was soon to become a battlefield for a religious war involving most of Europe's major powers. In 1690 King James lost the Battle of the Boyne to the Protestant William of Orange who went on to become king. Catholics subsequently suffered under the Penal Laws, Gaelic culture was driven underground, and the seeds were sewn for the struggle for Irish autonomy from England.

The 18th century ushered in a golden age for Dublin when the city flourished both physically and culturally. Parliament House (now the Bank of Ireland), Custom House, the Mansion House, the Four Courts and Marsh's Library were all built during this period. Jonathan Swift, the author of Gulliver's Travels, returned to the city in 1713 to become Dean of St Patrick's Cathedral, and Handel came to Dublin and gave the first performance of his Messiah in 1742.

This golden age was short lived, however. The Act of Union of 1800 brought Ireland into a United Kingdom with Britain, and the seat of political power moved from Dublin to Westminster. The city's aristocracy followed and Dublin lost much of its social and cultural sparkle.

A century of political turmoil followed. Daniel O'Connell helped to achieve Catholic emancipation in 1829 and, as a Catholic middle class developed, Dublin started to become a distinctly Irish city. The city managed to escape the worst effects of the potato famine which decimated much of Ireland in the late 1840's, and it expanded rapidly as migrants flooded in from the surrounding countryside. The effect of the famine on the country as a whole was devastating, however. Out of a population of 8.5 million, approximately one million starved to death and a further 1.5 million emigrated, mainly to Britain and North America. The famine years served to heighten anti-British sentiment, and an abortive rebellion by the Irish Republican Brotherhood in 1868 led to calls for Irish home rule.

The case for Irish autonomy was taken up in the English parliament at Westminster by the Protestant leader Charles Stewart Parnell. Parnell died in 1891, however, leaving a political vacuum which was eventually filled by two cultural movements, the Gaelic League which was set up to revive the Irish Language, and the Irish Literary Renaissance. William Butler Yeats played a pivotal role in restoring national pride with the foundation of the Abbey Theatre in 1904, giv-

Irish Famine memorial on Custom House Quay

ing prominence to playwrights such as Sean O'Casey and J M Synge. This cultural nationalism developed into political nationalism with the establishment of Sinn Féin (Ourselves Alone), a political movement which advocated a boycott of the English Parliament. With Britain engaged in the First World War, Sinn Féin organised the occupation of several strategic buildings around Dublin, and declared an Irish republic from its headquarters in the General Post Office on Easter Monday 1916.

The Easter Rising was quashed after six days of fighting with British forces, who numbered 20,000 troops, and 15 of the rebel leaders were later executed. A wave of public sympathy resulted, and Sinn Féin secured an overwhelming victory in the 1918 elections. A War of Independence between British and Irish republican armies soon followed and, after two years of fighting, Michael Collins signed a treaty in 1921 which resulted in the creation of the Irish Free State, comprising 26 of Ireland's 32 counties. The other six counties became known as Northern Ireland and remained within the United Kingdom. Collins said at the time that he was signing his own death warrant and he was proved right the following year.

The treaty caused division between different factions within Sinn Féin and a bitter Civil War broke out which lasted for a year and saw the destruction of much of the city. Eamon de Valera won the battle for political control of the new state, and a period of political and cultural conservatism ensued which lasted until the late 1950's.

Ireland was declared a republic in 1949, but it was not until the 1960's that Dublin started to look outwards. De Valera stepped down in 1959 to assume the figurehead role of Irish President, and a new Taoiseach (Prime Minister) Sean Lemass assumed power and began the process of modernisation and industrialisation. Perhaps the most defining moment in Dublin's recent history, however, was Ireland's admission to the European Economic Community in 1973.

Over the past thirty years, Ireland has been transformed from a predominantly agricultural country into a vibrant industrial economy. Dublin today is a modern European capital which boasts a young and well educated population which has proved attractive to many foreign investors. Church and government are becoming increasingly disentangled as evidenced by the 1995 referendum result in favour of divorce, and liberalisation of laws in relation to homosexuality and abortion.

The government's initiative in setting up the International Financial Services Centre in the heart of the city has succeeded in attracting many of the world's leading investment banks and Dublin now ranks as an important offshore financial centre. Ireland is also at the cutting edge in electronics and information technology, and Dublin has become a major European centre for the production of computer software. Economic progress over the past ten years has been startling, and the 'Celtic tiger' now produces a per capita income which exceeds that of the UK for the first time in Irish history.

This process of modernisation has brought problems as well as benefits, however. Drug culture and organised crime have prospered alongside the rest of the economy despite the war waged against them by government. Driving through the city tends to take place at a pace somewhere between slow and stop. Thankfully, though, Dublin retains much of its Georgian charm and grandeur. For a city with a population of around one million people, it is compact and intimate, with many of its attractions within walking distance of one another. This factor, together with its rich literary tradition and reputation for youthful exuberance and a friendly welcome, makes it one of the world's favourite tourist destinations.

Whether you are living here or merely passing through, the sections which follow will try to help you make the best of all that Dublin has to offer.

AIR TRAVEL

Dublin airport lies about 7 miles north of the city centre and is the international gateway for flights to many destinations across Europe and North America. Aer Lingus is Ireland's national airline, operating several domestic services out of Dublin in addition to its international routes. Aer Rianta, the airport managers, provide a comprehensive flight information service. Phone 844 4900 or access the airport web site on www.dublin-airport.com

International and domestic arrivals and departures share the same terminal building - arrivals are upstairs and departures are downstairs. Facilities include a foreign exchange counter in the arrivals area, a bank with extended opening hours, a cash machine, a post office and a very good tourist information office downstairs, as well as the usual array of bars, restaurants, cafés and shops. The tourist information office is a good first stop for directions and information, and it also offers a booking service for accommodation in exchange for a small fee of between £1 and £2.

Airlink, an express coach service, operates from outside the main terminal building into the city centre, stopping at Busárus, the central bus station, before going onto Connolly Railway Station and Heuston Railway Station. There are departures every twenty to thirty minutes from 6.40am to 11pm, and the single fare is £3 to Busárus and £3.50 to Heuston. Tickets can be bought from the driver and the journey normally takes around half an hour, depending on traffic.

Dublin Bus number 41 offers a cheaper alternative at approximately £1 for a single fare. It also departs from outside the main terminal building, but it takes considerably longer as it is a normal suburban service, stopping many times along its route to Eden Quay in the city centre.

A cab from the taxi rank in front of the terminal building will take you into the city centre for around £12 to £14 (no extra charge for the wise-cracking which tends to be the hallmark of Dublin taxi drivers).

Avis, Budget, Eurodollar and Hertz all have car hire desks at the airport, and a number of other operators will deliver cars for collection at the airport. Renting a car can be an expensive exercise in Ireland, mainly due to the high cost of insurance, and it usually pays to shop around. Pre-booking through a travel agent will avoid the disappointment of not being able to get hold of a car, which can sometimes happen during the summer months. Given that life behind the steering wheel in Dublin is often a frustrating one, and that the city centre is a very walkable one, you might well wonder why you bothered to hire a car in the first place!

FERRY SERVICES

There are two ferry ports in Dublin and your point of arrival will usually depend on your choice of ferry company.

Dublin Port, served mainly by Irish Ferries, is situated just a couple of miles from the city centre in a run down area of town known as the North Wall. Dublin Bus number 53 will take you the short distance into town.

Dún Laoghaire Port, served by Stena Line, is about seven miles south of the city centre and it is served by the DART train as well as Dublin bus numbers 7,8 and 45. The DART station is adjacent to the ferry terminal and the trains are fast and frequent. The terminal building has its own tourist information office which dispenses plenty of useful information and offers a booking service if you are in search of accommodation.

TRAINS

Irish rail services, including the DART, are operated by Iarnród Éireann (Irish Rail), and their Travel Centre at 35 Lower Abbey Street is a good place to gather information and make bookings. Phone 836 6222 for information on all services.

INTER CITY TRAINS

Rail journeys to Belfast, Sligo, Rosslare Harbour and Wexford start from Connolly Station (see page 25, grid reference H7) which is about ten minutes walk from O'Connell Bridge. Services to Ballina, Westport, Galway, Limerick, Killarney, Tralee, Cork and Waterford leave from Heuston Station (see page 24, grid reference E7) which is a short bus or taxi ride to the west of the city centre. A shuttle bus service called Stationlink runs every ten minutes between Connolly and Heuston Station, stopping at Busáras, the central bus station, on the way.

The rail network is adequate, covering most major towns and cities, but you will probably have to rely on bus services if you want to reach smaller towns. If you are expecting bullet trains, forget it. Services have been upgraded in recent years, most notably the Dublin to Belfast line, but you should still expect to take a couple of hours to cover a distance of 100 miles.

Travelling by train tends to cost more than going by bus but there are discounts available for students with an ISIC card (International Student Identity Card), and for anybody under the age of 26 who invests £7 in a European Youth Card (available from USIT at 19 Aston Quay). To take advantage of the discounts, however, it is necessary to stump up a further £7 for a Fare Stamp.

A selection of rail and/or bus passes is available if

you intend exploring the country as a whole. £75 will buy you an Irish Rover Rail Pass which allows 5 days of travel within any 15 day period on all Irish and Northern Irish inter city services, as well as DART and suburban rail services. An Emerald Card costs £105 and entitles you to 8 days travel within any fifteen day period, but coverage extends to Bus Eireann and Ulsterbus services. Phone 836 6222 for further information.

SUBURBAN TRAINS

Suburban services offer some very cheap travel. Trains leaving from Connolly Station head north as far as Dundalk, south as far as Arklow, and northwest as far as Mullingar. Services leaving from Heuston Station head west as far as Kildare (see route map opposite). Suburban trains use the same track as the DART but they make far fewer stops and therefore offer a good way of making day trips to places such as Malahide, Castletown House in the village of Celbridge, or Newgrange which is near Drogheda.

DART

The DART, or Dublin Area Rapid Transit, is a cheap but excellent electric rail service linking the city centre to various points along the coast of Dublin Bay, as far as Howth to the north, and Bray to the south (see the route map opposite). The main city centre stations are Pearse and Tara Street Stations which lie just south of the River Liffey, and Connolly Station which is just north of the river (see page 25, grid H7). Services operate every 15 minutes (every 5minutes during the rush hour) from around 6.30am to 11.30pm Monday-Saturday, and less frequently from 9.30am to 11pm on Sunday.

Single fares cost between 80p and £1.60 but a range of travel passes offer useful savings for frequent users. A one day travel ticket is valid for unlimited travel on the DART at a cost of £3.50. A one day family ticket costs £6 and allows unlimited DART travel for two adults and up to four children under the age of 16. Weekly tickets cost £11.50 per person and monthly tickets cost £43. A similar range of combined bus and rail tickets can also be purchased at very little additional cost (see page 68).

BUS SERVICES

DUBLIN BUS

Bus Átha Cliath (Dublin Bus) operates a comprehensive bus network which connects the city centre to all of the main suburbs of greater Dublin (see route maps on pages 66 & 67). Destinations and the service number are posted above the driver's window, with buses heading for the city centre displaying the Gaelic words "An Lár". Bus stops display the route numbers at the top and also provide additional route information on a revolving carousel. Travelling by bus is an inexact science, however, and timetables are therefore limited to the departure times from the terminus. Stops that display a "Set Down" sign are for buses which only let passengers off there, so don't wait around in the hope of getting on. The length of the queue at your stop is the best guide as to when the next bus is likely to arrive. Timetables can be obtained from Dublin Bus Head Office at 59 Upper O'Connell Street. For more detailed service information, telephone 873 4222.

Buses start running from 6am Monday-Saturday, and 10am on Sundays. Services usually run every 10 to 20 minutes on popular routes although you may have to wait for an hour on some of the quieter routes. Last buses leave the city centre at 11.30pm (see Nitelink on page 68 for special late night services).

Tickets can be bought on the bus, and you should try to have the exact fare ready as many routes operate an autofare system which means that the drivers do not have access to cash for security reasons. If you want to save time and money, however, a range of prepaid tickets can be purchased from Dublin Bus Head Office on Upper O'Connell Street, USIT on Aston Quay, the Tourist Office on Suffolk Street, and from many newsagents in the greater Dublin area. There are about 250 ticket agents in total and all have signs outside saying Dublin Bus Ticket Agent. Prepaid tickets are validated by a machine which you will find to your right as you board the bus. Some of these tickets allow combined access to bus, DART and suburban rail services. A selection is outlined below but take note that most pre-paid tickets are not valid for travel on Nitelink, Airlink, Ferry Services and Tours :

One Day Bus/Rail Ticket

Unlimited travel for one person : Travel by Dublin Bus costs £3.30; by DART costs £3.20; by bus & DART costs £4.50

One Day Family Bus/Rail Ticket

Unlimited travel for two adults and up to four children under the age of 16 : Travel by Dublin Bus costs £5.50; by Dart costs £5; by bus & DART costs £6.50

Three Day Rambler Ticket

Three days of unlimited travel for one person on Dublin Bus services and the Airlink bus service to and from the airport. Cost is £9.

Four Day Explorer Ticket

Unlimited travel on Dublin Bus, DART and suburban rail services for four consecutive days, from 9.45am Monday-Friday, and all day Saturday & Sunday. Cost is £10.

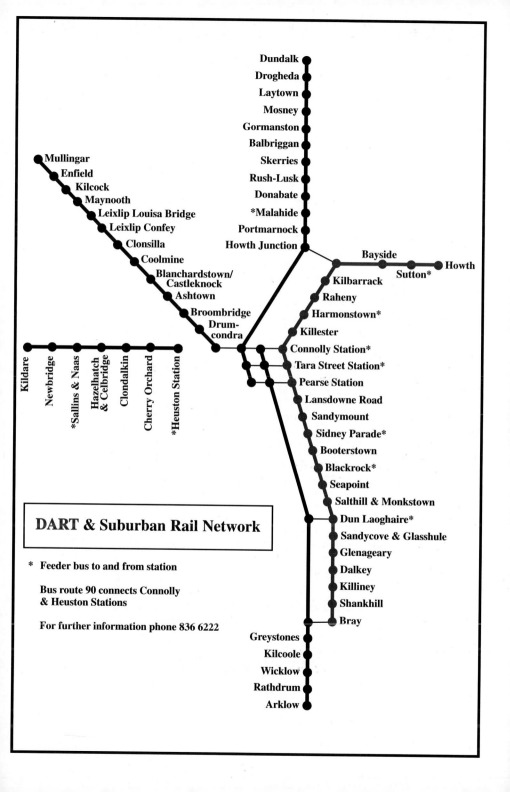

DART & Suburban Rail Network

Dundalk
Drogheda
Laytown
Mosney
Gormanston
Balbriggan
Skerries
Rush-Lusk
Donabate
*Malahide
Portmarnock
Howth Junction

Mullingar
Enfield
Kilcock
Maynooth
Leixlip Louisa Bridge
Leixlip Confey
Clonsilla
Coolmine
Blanchardstown/
Castleknock
Ashtown
Broombridge
Drum-
condra

Bayside
Sutton*
Howth
Kilbarrack
Raheny
Harmonstown*
Killester
Connolly Station*
Tara Street Station*
Pearse Station
Lansdowne Road
Sandymount
Sidney Parade*
Booterstown
Blackrock*
Seapoint
Salthill & Monkstown
Dun Laoghaire*
Sandycove & Glasshule
Glenageary
Dalkey
Killiney
Shankhill
Bray

Kildare
Newbridge
*Sallins & Naas
Hazelhatch & Celbridge
Clondalkin
Cherry Orchard
*Heuston Station

Greystones
Kilcoole
Wicklow
Rathdrum
Arklow

* Feeder bus to and from station

Bus route 90 connects Connolly
& Heuston Stations

For further information phone 836 6222

CITY CENTRE BUS STOPS

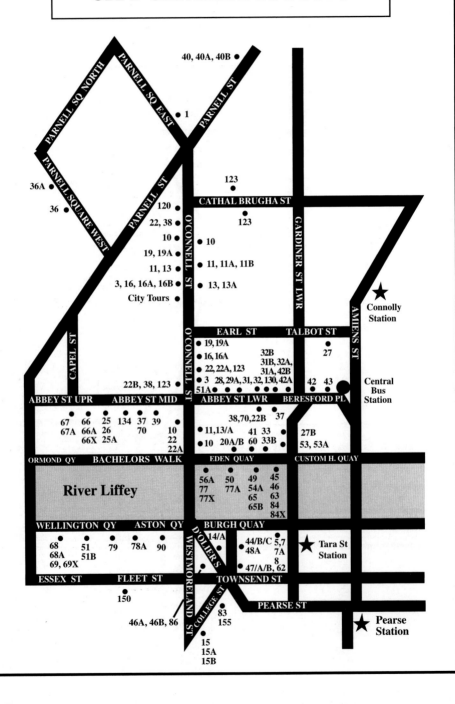

DUBLIN BUS ROUTE NETWORK

31 Operate to or via city centre
(75) Do not operate via city centre

Swords
33, 41, 41B
41C, 43, (230)

Malahide
32A, 42
(102, 230)

Kinsealy
42, 43

Portmarnock
32, 32A
(102, 230)

Dublin Airport
41, 41B, 41C, (300)

Darndale
27, 42, (101)

Ballymun
13, 36, 36A
(17A,220)

Santry
16,16A,16B
33, 33B, 41
41B, 41C
(300)

Coolock
27 (17A)

Baldoyle
32, 32A
32B, (102)

Sutton
31, 31A, 31B

Blanchardstown
38, 39, 70
(76A,237,239)

Beaumont
27B, 51A
(101, 103, 300)

Edenmore
42A/B (101)

Kilbarrack
29A, 31, 31A, 31B
32A, 32B, (17A)

Howth
31, 31B

Clonsilla
39, (239)

Finglas
134, 40, 40A, 40B
(17A, 103, 220)

Glasnevin
13, 19, 134

Whitehall
3,16,16A,33,41
41A,41B,41C,(103)

Artane
27, 27B, 42
42B, 43

Raheny
29A, 31, 31A
31B, 32, 32A, 32B

Howth Summit
31B

Castleknock
37, 38
(237,239)

Ashtown
37, 38, 39, 70

Drumcondra
3,11,11A,16,13A

Marino
123

Killester
29A, 31/A/B
32/A/B, 42A
(103)

Dollymount
130

Lucan
25/A, 66/A
67, 67A

Cabra
120, 121, 122

Phibsboro
10,19/A, 22,
134, 38, 120

Fairview
20A/B,130

Clontarf
130

Phoenix Park

Palmerston
25/A, 26, 66/A/B
67, 67A(18)

Chapelizod
25,25A,26,66
66A/B,67,67A

Islandbridge
25,25A,26,68,69

Ringsend
1, 3

Ballyfermot
78A, 79, (18
76, 76A, 76B)

Kilmainham
68, 69, 78A

City Centre

Sandymount
3, (18)

Neilstown
51, (76/A/B, 210)

Cherry Orchard
78A, (18,76/A/B)

Inchicore
51, 51B
68, 69

Dolphin's Barn
19, 50, 56A, 77/A
122, 150, (17, 210)

Ballsbridge
5,7/A,8,45,(18)

Drimnagh
22,22A,123

Harold's Cross
16,16A,49,49A
54,65,65B

Ranelagh
11/A,13B,48A
62, 66, (18)

Donnybrook
10, 46/A/B

Clondalkin
51,51B,68,69
(76/A/B, 210)

Walkinstown
56A, 77, 77A
155, (18)

Crumlin
50, 56A, 77
77A, 150, (210)

Rathmines
14/A, 15/B
83, (18)

Clonskeagh
11/A, 62, (17)

Booterstown
5, 7, 7A, 8, 45

Kilnamanagh
50, 77, (202)

Greenhills
50, 54A, 77

Kimmage
15A, 54A
155, (17)

Terenure
15/A/B, 16/A
49/A, (17)

Rathgar
15A/B
47/A/B

Milltown
44,44B,44C
48A, 86

Blackrock
7, 7A, 8, 45
(17, 114)

Rathfarnham
16, 16A, 47A
47B, (17)

Churchtown
14, 14A

Mount Merrion
5, 46/A/B, 63

Monkstown
7A, 8

Dun Laoghaire
7, 7A, 8, 46A
(45A,59,75,111)

Tallaght
49, 49A, 50, 54A
65, 65B, 77, 77A
(75, 76, 76A, 76B
201, 202)

Firhouse
49, 49A
(75)

Templeogue
15B, 49, 49A
65, 65B

Dundrum
44, 44B, 44C
48A, (17, 750)

Goatstown
62

Sillorgan
46/A, 63, 84
86, (75)

Kill of the Grange
46A

Dalkey
8

Jobstown
77, (201)

Ballyboden
47a, 47B, (161)

Ballinteer
14, 14A
48A, (75)

Sandyford
5, 44, 62
(75,114,115)

Deans Grange
45, 46A, (75)

Sallynoggin
7,7A,(45A,111)

Oldbawn
49,49A, (75, 76B)

Cornelscourt
45, 46, 84, 86

Killiney
(59)

Cabinteely
45, 46, 84, 86

Rockbrook
(161)

Tibradden
(161)

Foxrock
63, 86

Carrickmines
63, 86

Ballybrack
7, 46, (45A, 111)

Stepaside
44

Enniskerry
44

Bray
45, 84, (45A)

Weekly Bus/Rail Tickets

Seven days of unlimited travel starting on Sunday. Photograph required. Travel by Dublin Bus costs £13; by DART costs £10.50; by bus & DART costs £15.50

Monthly tickets are available if you are living in Dublin, and worthwhile price reductions are available to students with an ISIC Card and an £8 Travelsave stamp which can be purchased from USIT at 19 Aston Quay.

LATE NIGHT BUSES

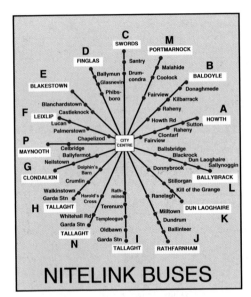

NITELINK BUSES

Dublin Bus operate a late-night express bus service called Nitelink which will get you from the city centre to a wide range of suburban destinations on Thursday, Friday, and Saturday nights (nightly over the Christmas period). Buses depart from College Street, D'Olier Street, and Westmoreland Street (see page 25, grid H7) on the hour from midnight until 3am and the price of a ticket is £2.50 (The route to Maynooth departs at 1am and 3am and the fare is £4). Travel passes are not valid on Nitelink buses. For further information contact 873 4222.

AIRPORT BUS

Dublin Bus operate a coach service called Airlink which follows a route between Dublin Airport (bus stop number 1 outside the arrivals hall) and Heuston Rail Station, stopping at Connolly Rail Station and Busáras Central Bus Station on the way (see page 25,

grid H7). The single fare costs £3 into the city centre and £3.50 if you are travelling on to Heuston Station. Phone 873 4222 for further information.

BUS EIREANN

Bus Éireann (Irish Bus) is the national bus company, operating routes which cover the whole of Ireland. Fares, as a rule, are cheaper than going by train. All buses depart from Busáras, the central bus station, which is situated behind Custom House on the north side of the river (see page 25, grid H7). Tickets and information are available at Busárus or from the Bus Eireann desk in the Dublin Tourism Centre on Suffolk Street. Phone 836 6111 for more information.

BUS TOURS

Dublin Bus operate a range of daily tours all year round, but with increased frequency during the summer months. The Dublin City Tour (from an open-topped double decker, weather permitting!) lasts for an hour and fifteen minutes and stops at the Dublin Writers Museum, Trinity College, the National Gallery, St Stephen's Green, Dublin Tourism Centre, Dublin Castle, St Patrick's Cathedral, Christ Church, Guinness Hopstore, the National Museum, and the Old Jameson Distillery. The tour runs at frequent intervals, normally every ten minutes, between 9.30am and 6.30pm. Tickets, which cost £6 per adult and £3 per child under 14, are valid all day and you can hop on and off the bus as the fancy takes you.

The Grand Dublin Tour lasts about three hours and includes the Custom House, Kilmainham Jail, the Royal Hospital, and the Phoenix Park. The tour departs daily at 10.15am and 2.15pm and tickets cost £8 per adult and £4 per child under 14. If you would like to see beyond the city, a tour of the north Dublin coastline operates during the summer, and a tour of the south Dublin coastline runs during both winter and summer. Both tours last about three hours. All tours start and finish outside the Dublin Bus HQ at 59 Upper O'Connell Street. Phone 873 4222 for more details.

Bus Eireann offer a wide range of sightseeing tours starting from about £15 per person. Destinations include Glendalough & the Wicklow mountains, Newgrange & the Boyne Valley, Kilkenny, Waterford & New Ross, and the Mountains of Mourne. Phone 836 6111 for further details.

Gray Line offer a range of summertime tours both around Dublin and farther afield to places such as Newgrange, Malahide Castle, Powerscourt Gardens and Newbridge House. Night time tours incorporate an evening of Irish cabaret. Phone 605 7705 for information or go to their reservations desk in the Dublin Tourism Centre in Suffolk Street.

If you want to tour Ireland by bus, CIE offer a wide

range of tours from Busárus Central Bus Station. For more information, contact CIE Tours, 35 Lower Abbey Street. Phone 836 3333

TAXIS

Dublin Taxis can be hailed on the street or obtained at one of the many taxi ranks which can be found outside leading hotels, train and bus stations, and at strategic city centre locations such as O'Connell Street, Aston Quay, Eden Quay, College Green, St Stephen's Green and Lansdowne Road. The queues at these ranks can seem a bit daunting at times, but bear in mind that it can often feel like mission impossible getting hold of a cab on the street, especially late at night when the clubs are closing.

Fares are metered for journeys within 10 miles of the city centre, but there are numerous add-ons for additional passengers, luggage, and unsociable hours. Fares to outlying destinations should be agreed with the driver beforehand, but you should expect to pay about £1 per mile. Look in the Golden Pages under "Taxicabs" if you want to phone for a taxi, or try All Fives Taxi on 455 5555, All Sevens Taxi on 677 777, or City Cabs who can provide wheelchair access on 872 7272.

CAR HIRE

Renting a car in Ireland is usually an expensive exercise but, if you want to explore the country beyond Dublin, a car is a necessity as the public transport system has some severe limitations. Cost will typically be somewhere between £250 and £350 pounds per week depending on the car, the size of the hire company, and the time of year. Despite the cost, availability can sometimes be a problem during the summer months so it is advisable to book in advance.

Budget Rent A Car   `17 H5`
Dublin Airport - phone 844 5919. 151 Drumcondra Road Lower - phone 677 6971

Dan Dooley Car & Van Rentals   `25 H8`
42/43 Westland Row- phone 677 2723

Hertz Rent-a-Car   `31 H9`
Dublin Airport -phone 844 5466. 149 Leeson Street Upper -phone 660 2255.

Murrays Europcar   `25 H8`
Baggot Street Bridge - phone 668 1777

Thrifty Rent-a-Car   `25 G8`
14 Duke Street - phone 679 9420

BICYCLE HIRE

Dublin is pretty flat and well suited, therefore, to exploring on bike, although a good lock and a brave heart in traffic are both very important. If you want to travel beyond Dublin by bike, Raleigh Rent-a-Bike have numerous agencies around the country, and they offer one-way rentals between different outlets. Hiring a bike typically costs around £8 per day, or £35 per week. City Cycle Tours offer daily tours of the city by bike from 1A Temple Lane. Phone 671 5606 for details.

C. Harding for Bicycles   `25 G7`
(Raleigh Rent-a-Bike Agent)
30 Bachelor's Walk - phone 873 2455. You can park your bike here for 50p for the first hour and £1 for the rest of the day.

Rent-a-Bike Head Office   `17 H6`
58 Lower Gardiner Street - phone 872 5399

Dublin Bike Hire   `17 G6`
27 North Great George's Street - phone 878 8473

WALKING TOURS

Dublin Tourism publish a couple of useful guides on touring : The Dublin Touring Guide which suggests five different city walks and a number of excursions out of Dublin, and The Rock 'n' Stroll Guide to Dublin which takes you on a tour of various places around the city which have played a significant role in the development of the numerous famous bands to come out of Dublin in recent years.

Of the organised walking tours, the most informative are conducted by history graduates from Trinity College who will take you on a two hour historical tour of the city and share their considerable historical knowledge along the way. The tour takes in Trinity College, Dublin Castle, Christ Church, St Audoen's and the Norman walls. Tours leave from the front gate at Trinity at noon on Saturday and Sunday. Cost is £4 per head. Phone 845 0241 for group bookings.

If you like to combine walking with drinking, the Dublin Literary Pub Crawl offers a very entertaining tour of some southside pubs associated with Dublin's legion of thirsty writers. The tour starts at The Duke on Duke Street. Phone 454 0228 for information. The Musical Pub Crawl, on the other hand, aims to enhance your knowledge of Irish music, starting off upstairs at Oliver St John Gogarty's in Temple Bar. Phone 478 0191. See page 89 for more detail.

Some would argue that it's due to the free advertising that Ireland gains from repeatedly winning the Eurovision Song Contest, but finding a bed when visiting Dublin can be difficult at times, especially at weekends and at any time during the height of the tourist season. For a capital city, Dublin is not over endowed with hotels, and although more are opening all the time, supply has not managed to keep up with demand in recent years. The golden rule, therefore, is to book your accommodation, either directly or through an agent, before you arrive. A couple of weeks in advance should be enough notice during the quieter times of year, but a month or two might be required if you want to stay in one of the more popular hotels during the summer months.

If you have acted on impulse, however, and find yourself in Dublin with no accommodation booked, reservations can be made for around £1 per person at one of the following tourist information centres: Dublin Airport, Dun Laoghaire Harbour, Suffolk Street, Baggot Street Bridge, and at the Square Towncentre in Tallaght. Telephone bookings can be made with a credit card by phoning 605 7777. The fee for this service is £3. A deposit is payable at the time of reservation, but this amount is deducted when the final bill is being settled. Touch-screen booking services operate on a 24 hour basis at Dublin Airport, Dun Laoghaire Ferry Terminal, and outside Dublin Tourism Centre on Suffolk Street.

An alternative booking service is offered by Bedfinders. Reservations can be made by phoning 670 4704. There is a booking fee of around £1 per person and a deposit of 10% is payable. All participating premises are vetted by Bedfinders, including some which are not recognised by Bord Failte.

A small cross section of accommodation is listed below. In an effort to keep things simple, the accommodation has been categorised as 'expensive', 'moderate' or 'budget'. Specific prices are not given as rates often vary according to the time of year and most of the more expensive establishments offer special deals, usually relating to weekend stays. Some of the city's guest houses offer rather more interesting accommodation than many of the hotels and a couple of the better ones are included in the moderate category.

Family-run B&B's form the bedrock of budget accommodation, costing around £20 per person sharing, but most are located in the outer suburbs of the city. Premises approved by Bord Failte display a shamrock sign and bookings can be made directly or through the tourist information centres mentioned above. If you are looking for something cheap, but close to the city centre, hostels offer a realistic alternative now that they have shaken off their down-at-heel image. Some have conventional bedrooms but most offer clean and comfortable dorm-style rooms with shared bathrooms. They are inspected and registered by Bord Failte but are not graded. Price normally depends on how many are sharing, but rates are typically £8-£14 per person per night.

During the summer months, from about mid-June until mid-September, it is possible to book university accommodation at Trinity College which is right in the heart of the city centre, at UCD to the south of the city centre, and at Dublin City University to the north. Self catering and bed & breakfast accommodation is available and prices start from around £20 per person per night for a single room.

All Dublin hotels are inspected by Bord Failte (the Irish Tourist Board), and each is given a star rating, from one to five stars, to reflect the standard of the accommodation and the facilities available. Guest houses, which tend to be less expensive than hotels, are rated on a similar system, from one to four stars. The appropriate star rating is listed below after the name of each establishment. The hotels and guest houses selected tend to provide rooms with en suite bathroom facilities as standard.

For a more comprehensive list, the Ireland Accommodation Guide, published by Bord Failte, gives details of accommodation throughout Ireland which has been approved by the Tourist Board. The guide costs £5 and is available at all tourist offices.

Georgian splendour at the Shelbourne Hotel

Accommodation Prices

Expensive: Expect to pay in the region of £80 to £120 per night per person sharing. Cheaper rates are often available at weekends.

Moderate: Expect to pay between £30 to £60 per night per person sharing. Once again, cheaper weekend rates may be available.

Budget: Most budget accommodation costs between £15 and £30 per night per person sharing.

EXPENSIVE

BERKELEY COURT HOTEL***　`32 J9`
Lansdowne Road, Ballsbridge
Phone 660 1711. 190 bedrooms
A rather uninspiring exterior despite its pleasant setting, but the very plush interior tries hard to make amends.

BURLINGTON HOTEL**　`31 H9`
Upper Leeson Street, Dublin 4
Phone 660 5222. 451 bedrooms
Dublin's largest hotel, and another uninspiring exterior, but inside is warm, comfortable and friendly, with a lobby which teems with life throughout the day and long into the night. Entry to the hotel nightclub, Annabel's, is free to guests.

CLARENCE HOTEL***　`25 G7`
6-8 Wellington Quay, Temple Bar
Phone 670 9000. 50 bedrooms
Probably the trendiest hotel in town, largely due to the fact that it's owned by the rock band, U2. The hotel restaurant, the Tea Rooms, and its nightclub, the Kitchen, are rated among the best in Dublin. The penthouse suite with its roof-top hot-tub overlooking the Liffey is a good place to impress the new woman or man in your life, or simply a good place to put some new life into the one you already have.

SHELBOURNE HOTEL***　`25 H8`
27 St. Stephen's Green
Phone 676 6471. 164 bedrooms
This is the grand old lady of Dublin hotels. Georgian elegance is the hallmark of the Shelbourne although only the very finest, and most expensive, bedrooms get to enjoy the view over St Stephen's Green.

WESTBURY HOTEL***　`25 G7`
Henry Street, Dublin 2
Phone 679 1122. 163 bedrooms & 40 suites
Located just off Grafton Street, the Westbury is one of Dublin's leading hotels and an ideal base from which to explore the finest shops in the city, and much more.

MODERATE

BEWLEY'S HOTEL*　`25 G7`
19/20 Fleet Street, Dublin 2
Phone 670 8122 . 70 bedrooms
Its location on the edge of Temple Bar makes Bewley's a good choice if you wish to sample the vibrancy of Dublin life, by day and by night.

CENTRAL HOTEL*　`25 G8`
1-5 Exchequer Street, Dublin 2
Phone 679 7302. 70 bedrooms
Refurbished 19th century building, close to all main shopping areas and very conveniently located for many of the city's best bars and restaurants.

JURY'S CHRISTCHURCH INN*　`25 G8`
Christchurch Place, Dublin 8
Phone 454 0000. 182 rooms
The distinguishing characteristic of a Jury's Inn is that guests pay a flat rate per room, rather than paying per person in the room. This has proved to be a popular and successful formula which Jury's has developed throughout Ireland and Great Britain. Each room can accommodate up to three adults, or two adults and two children. Jury's Inns tend to be large, modern, three star establishments with good facilities, and this one benefits from a pleasant location opposite Christ Church Cathedral, only a few minutes walk from Temple Bar. Expect to pay around £60 for a room, excluding breakfast, although this rate can double for special events such as a rugby international weekend. Jury's attract a lot of business, so try to book well in advance.

JURY'S CUSTOM HOUSE INN*　`25 H7`
Custom House Quay
Phone 607 5000. 234 rooms
Overlooking the Liffey, next to the International Financial Services Centre, the format is the same as its sister hotel in Christchurch : new hotel, all rooms en suite with colour TV, telephone and tea/coffee making facilities, and a fixed charge of around £60 per room.

Trinity College - a peaceful oasis in the heart of the city

Each room can take up to three adults, or two adults and two children. Prices double for special events such as rugby international weekends.

STAUNTONS ON THE GREEN*** `25 H8`
83 St. Stephen's Green
Phone 478 2300. 26 rooms
Elegant Georgian guest house overlooking the Green. Own private garden and an enviable location which is handy for just about everything.

THE TOWNHOUSE `17 H6`
47-48 Lower Gardiner St, Dublin 1
Phone 878 8808. 64 rooms
Refurbished Georgian guest house. Formerly home to the 19th century playwrights Dion Boucicault and Lafacadio Hearn which helps to explain why each room bears a literary name.

BUDGET

AVALON HOUSE `25 G8`
55 Aungier Street, Dublin 2
Phone 475 0001
Well run hostel accommodation for 150 guests in single, twin, four and multi-bedded rooms. Convenient location within easy walking distance of St Stephen's Green, Grafton Street and Temple Bar.

DUBLIN CITY UNIVERSITY `7 G3`
Glasnevin, Dublin 9
Phone 704 5736. Approx 500 rooms
Single and double bedrooms in modern apartment blocks located a couple of miles to the north of the city centre. Rooms are either en suite or share a bathroom with one other. Price includes access to the campus facilities. Mid-June to mid-September.

OLIVER ST JOHN GOGARTY'S `25 G7`
18-21 Anglesea Street, Temple Bar
Phone 671 1822
Modern hostel which caters for individuals and groups of up to ten people sharing. Accommodation includes 4-person rooftop apartments with kitchen, TV and washing machine.

GLOBETROTTERS TOURIST HOSTEL `17 H6`
46/48 Lower Gardiner St, Dublin 1
Phone 873 5893
Converted Georgian town houses providing a high standard of accommodation which includes a mixture of dormitories and twin and triple rooms.

KINLAY HOUSE `25 G8`
2-12 Lord Edward Street
Phone 679 6644. 33 bedrooms + 20 dorms
One of the largest and busiest hostels in the city, its location close to Temple Bar helps to maintain a lively atmosphere throughout the year. Accommodation is provided in twin, four, and six bedded rooms. Facilities include a cafe and a laundry, and prices include continental breakfast.

TRINITY COLLEGE `25 G7`
College Green
Phone 608 1177. Approx 600 rooms
Not as cheap an option as one might expect, but don't forget that the historic city centre location is factored into the price, and parking is free. Accommodation ranges from rather monastic single rooms which overlook the cobbles and cost around £30, to modern self catering apartments on the edge of campus. Mid-June to mid-September.

UNIVERSITY COLLEGE DUBLIN `38 K12`
Belfield, Dublin 4
Phone 269 7111. Approx 1200 rooms
Modern self-catering accommodation set in the landscaped grounds of Dublin's largest university which is located about three miles south of the city centre. Individual rooms and apartments. Mi-June to mid-September.

ABBEY THEATRE
See page 82.

THE ARK CHILDREN'S CULTURAL CENTRE
11A Eustace Street, Temple Bar `25 G7`
Phone 670 7788
The stated aim of the Ark is to promote and develop high quality cultural work by children, for children and about children. Various programmes run throughout the year making use of the building's theatre, gallery and workshop, but most require advance booking. Interested adults can drop in between 5pm and 7pm every Thursday to find out more about the work of the Ark.

ARTHOUSE MULTIMEDIA CENTRE FOR THE ARTS
Curved Street, Temple Bar `25 G7`
Phone 605 6800
ARTHOUSE is one of the flagship projects in the cultural redevelopment of the Temple Bar district. One of its main functions is to train artists in the use of computer technology. Facilities include a multimedia production unit, exhibition space, a cyber café, and a library which maintains a computerised database of contemporary Irish artists which can be accessed via the Internet. Their web site address is http://www.arthouse.ie *Opening Times: Mon-Fri 10am-5.30pm.*

BANK OF IRELAND
2 College Green, Dublin 2 `25 G7`
Phone 677 6801
One of Dublin's most impressive buildings, the Bank of Ireland began life as Parliament House in 1729 but, when the Act of Union was passed in 1800, the government of Ireland was transferred to London, and the building was later sold and converted into a bank. The main banking hall now occupies what was once the House of Commons chamber but the House of Lords chamber has survived in tact. Items of interest include the parliamentary mace, an impressive Waterford crystal chandelier dating from 1765, and two large 18th century tapestries depicting the Battle of the Boyne in 1690 and the Siege of Derry in 1689. The building can be visited free of charge from Monday to Friday during banking hours, and there are guided tours of the House of Lords every Tuesday at 10.30am, 11.30am and 1.45pm.

BANK OF IRELAND ARTS CENTRE
Foster Place, Dublin 2 `25 G7`
Phone 671 1488
Originally the bank armoury, the centre is now home to the Story of Banking Museum which chronicles the role played by the Bank of Ireland in the economic and social development of Ireland over the past 200 years. It also traces the history of the College Green building back to when it used to be the Irish Houses of Parliament. The centre also plays host to temporary exhibitions and is a regular venue for concerts of classical music. *Opening Times: Tues-Fri 10am-4pm. Admission charge is £1.50 per adult.*

BEACHES
The suburban rail system and the DART put quite a few sandy beaches within easy reach of the city centre. These include Malahide and Portmarnock to the north and Sandymount to the south. See "Swimming" on page 86.

CASINO AT MARINO
off Malahide Road, Dublin 3 `18 K4`
Phone 833 1618
This isn't a casino but it *is* an architectural gem, built in the 1760's as a pleasure house in the grounds of Marino Estate. Marino House, however, was demolished in 1920 and much of the estate was sold off for development. Fortunately, the Casino, which actually means "small house", survives as a glorious folly. Tours of the building are conducted daily from 9.30am-6.30pm between June and September; May & Oct, Mon-Sun 10am-5pm; Feb/March/Apr/Nov, Sun & Wed 12noon-4pm. Admission charge is £2 per person.

CENTRAL LIBRARY
See page 79.

CHESTER BEATTY LIBRARY & GALLERY OF ORIENTAL ART
See page 79.

CHRIST CHURCH CATHEDRAL
Christchurch Place, Dublin 8 `25 G8`
Phone 677 8099
The Cathedral of the Holy Trinity, or Christ Church as it is commonly known, is one of two Church of Ireland cathedrals in Dublin and the city's oldest building with sections dating back to 1172. The cathedral was founded by Sitric, the Norse King of Dublin, in 1038 but it was the Normans, led by Strongbow, who rebuilt the original wooden structure in stone. Much of the building collapsed due to subsidence in 1562 and most of what is seen above ground today is the result of major restoration work carried out during the 19th century. The vast crypt, however, dates back to the Norman period and it houses many relics and curiosities includ-

Statues of Neptune, Mercury, Plenty, Industry and Hope

building's classical facade is built from Portland stone and is best viewed from across the river. The rooftop statues of Neptune, Mercury, Plenty and Industry represent various aspects of transport and trade, and the statue on top of the central copper dome represents Hope. Although the building was ravaged by fire during the War of Independence in 1921, it was later restored. A visitor centre is located in and around the Dome area of the building. *Opening Times: Mon-Fri 10am-5pm, Sat & Sun 2pm-5pm (closed Mon/Tues/Sat from November to mid-March). Admission charge is £1 per adult.*

DUBLIN CASTLE `25 G7`
Dame Street, Dublin 2
Phone 677 7129
Large parts of Dublin Castle have been rebuilt over the centuries and the building today is more palatial in style than one might expect. The original castle was built on the orders of King John in 1204 on the site of an earlier Viking fortification, remnants of which have been preserved and are on view at the 'Undercroft'. Dublin Castle was at the heart of British military and administrative rule in Ireland for 700 years and it was used during that time as a military fortress, a prison, record office, courts of law and residence of the British viceroys of Ireland. The fact that the statue of Justice above the main gate stands with her back turned towards the city was seen by Dubliners as an apt symbol of British rule. Presidents of Ireland are now invested in the castle and its facilities are used to host European Union conferences and summits. The castle's State Apartments, Undercroft and Chapel Royal are open to visitors and the Chester Beatty Library and Gallery of Oriental Art has recently taken up residence in the refurbished barracks. *Opening Times: Mon-Fri 10am-5pm, Sat-Sun 2pm-5pm. Admission charge is £2.50 per adult.*

DUBLIN CIVIC MUSEUM
See page 79.

DUBLIN TOURISM CENTRE `25 G7`
Suffolk Street, Dublin 2
Phone 605 7755
Impressive new premises housed in the former church of St Andrew. Services include tourist information and accommodation reservations for the whole of Ireland, a bookstore, gift shop, café, bureau de change, and booking facilities for Bus Eireann Tours, Grayline Tours, and Argus Rent-a-Car. Other Information Centres can be found on Baggot Street Bridge, at Dublin Airport, Dun Laoghaire Port and at the Square Towncentre in Tallaght.

ing a mummified cat and rat. Choral Evensong takes place at 6pm on Wednesdays and Thursdays (except in July and August), 5pm on Saturdays and 3.30pm on Sundays. *Opening Times: Mon-Sun 10am-5pm. A donation of £1 per adult is requested.*

CITY HALL `25 G8`
Lord Edward Street
Phone 679 6111
Completed in 1779 as the Royal Exchange, the building became the centre of municipal government in 1852. The City Hall's most striking feature is its interior rotunda with a central mosaic depicting the city's coat of arms, and a series of frescos depicting the heraldic arms of the four Irish provinces and various aspects of Dublin. *Opening Times: Mon-Fri 10am-1pm & 2.15pm-5pm. Admission is free.*

CUSTOM HOUSE `25 H7`
Custom House Quay, Dublin 1
Phone 878 7660
One of Dublin's finest Georgian buildings, Custom House has been a familiar part of the city skyline since it was completed in 1791. Designed by James Gandon, who was also responsible for the Four Courts, the

DUBLIN'S VIKING ADVENTURE `25 G7`
Essex Street West, Dublin 8
Phone 679 6040
Dublin's Viking Adventure is situated near to the Civic Offices of Dublin Corporation which were built, amid a storm of protest, on Dublin's most important Viking site at Wood Quay. The tour begins on a 'boat' which sails back in time until you arrive in the narrow streets of Viking Dublin where you are able to chat with a few of the locals, watch them at work, and experience sounds and smells from a thousand years ago. Artefacts excavated from the Wood Quay site are also on display. *Opening Times: March-October, Tues-Sat 10am-4.30pm. Admission charge is £4.95 per adult.*

DVBLINIA `25 G8`
Christ Church, St Michael's Hill, Dublin 8
Phone 679 4611
Housed in the old Synod Hall beside Christ Church Cathedral, Dvblinia tells the story of medieval Dublin from the arrival of Strongbow and the Anglo-Normans in 1170 to the dissolution of the monasteries by Henry VIII in 1540. Various displays, a scale model of the medieval city and a collection of artefacts from the Wood Quay site all help to bring this period of history to life. A personal 'Acoustiguide', available in five languages, helps to explain the various exhibits. The admission price includes a visit to Christ Church Cathedral which is linked by an archway to the old Synod Hall. *Opening Times: April-Sept Mon-Sun 10am-5pm; Oct-March, Mon-Sat 11am-4pm, Sun 10am-4.30pm. Admission is £3.95 per adult.*

DUBLIN WRITERS MUSEUM
See page 79.

DUBLIN ZOO `15 D6`
Phoenix Park
Phone 677 1425
The Zoo was founded in 1830 making it the third oldest in the world. It is situated in the Phoenix Park, within easy reach of the main entrance on Parkgate Street. The Zoo places a heavy emphasis on the breeding of endangered species, but there is plenty to see, including a daily feeding programme for gorillas, polar bears, reptiles, sea-lions and elephants. New areas include the 'World of Cats', the 'World of Primates' and the 'Fringes of the Arctic'. *Opening Times : Mon-Sat 9.30am-6pm; Sun 10.30am-6pm. Admission charge is £5.90 per adult, £3.20 per child.*

FOUR COURTS `24 F7`
Inns Quay, Dublin 7
Home to the Irish law courts since 1796, the Four

The hustle and bustle of Grafton Street

Courts building has much in common with Custom House. Both were designed by James Gandon and both required major restoration following fire damage suffered during the turbulence of 1921 and 1922. The public is admitted only when the courts are in session.

THE FRY MODEL RAILWAY MUSEUM
See page 79.

THE GAA MUSEUM
See page 79.

THE GALLERY OF PHOTOGRAPHY
See page 79.

GENERAL POST OFFICE `25 G7`
O'Connell Street, Dublin 1
Phone 705 7000
The General Post Office was built in 1815 and is best known for its role as rebel headquarters during the 1916 Easter Rising. All but destroyed in the ensuing battle, it re-opened in 1929 and continues in public use today.

GRAFTON STREET `25 G8`
Grafton Street is Dublin's premier shopping street and,

as such, it is described on page 87. Even if you are allergic to shopping, however, it is still worth taking a leisurely stroll along this pedestrianised thoroughfare which also acts as an open air venue for some amusing street theatre, many talented buskers, and an array of other colourful characters.

GUINNESS HOP STORE   `24 F8`
Crane Street, Dublin 8
Phone 453 6700
Situated close to the famous St James's Gate Brewery, the Guinness Hop Store houses the 'World of Guinness' exhibition which uses museum displays and an audio-visual presentation to tell the story of Guinness. The entry fee entitles you to a glass of the black stuff in the visitors' bar. *Opening Times : Apr-Sept, Mon-Sat 9.30am-5pm, Sun 10.30am-4.30pm; Oct-Mar, Mon-Sat 9.30am-4pm, Sun 12noon-4pm. Admission charge is £4 per adult.*

HA'PENNY BRIDGE   `25 G7`
Bachelor's Walk
The Ha'penny Bridge is a cast-iron footbridge which spans the Liffey, providing a convenient gateway to Temple Bar if you are crossing from the north side of the river. Built in 1816, the halfpenny toll no longer applies today!

HERALDIC MUSEUM & GENEALOGICAL OFFICE
See page 79.

HUGH LANE MUNICIPAL GALLERY
See page 80.

IRISH FILM CENTRE
See pages

IRISH MUSEUM OF MODERN ART
See page 80.

THE JAMES JOYCE CENTRE
See page 80.

THE JAMES JOYCE MUSEUM
See page 80.

KILMAINHAM GAOL
See page 80.

LEINSTER HOUSE   `25 H8`
Kildare Street
Leinster House is the seat of Irish government, home to Dáil Éireann (House of Representatives) which comprises 166 elected TD's, and Seanad Éireann (Senate) to which 60 senators are appointed. Erected in 1745, the building is only open to the public when parliament is not sitting.

MALAHIDE CASTLE
Malahide (See page 65)
Phone 846 2184
This charming castle has been both a fortress and the family home of the Talbots for nearly 800 years, right up until the last Lord Talbot died in 1973. The architecture reflects many different styles, and the interior is enhanced by an impressive collection of period furniture and an historic series of Irish portraits, most of which are on loan from the National Gallery. The castle stands in 250 acres of park land which is also open to the public. *Opening Times: Apr-Oct, Mon-Sat 10am-5pm, Sun11am-6pm; Nov-Mar, Mon-Fri 10am-5pm, Sat & Sun 2pm-5pm. Admission charge is £3.10 per adult.*

MANSION HOUSE   `25 H8`
Dawson Street
The Mansion House has been the official residence of the Lord Mayor of Dublin since 1715. The first Irish Parliament met here in 1919 to adopt the Declaration of Independence. The house is not open to the public.

MARSH'S LIBRARY
See page 80.

MERRION SQUARE   `25 H8`
The best preserved Georgian square in Dublin and, as the wall plaques indicate, home to many historic figures including Daniel O'Connell and W B Yeats. The public gardens in the centre of the square are a hidden gem.

NATIONAL BOTANIC GARDENS   `16 F4`
Glasnevin, Dublin 9
Phone 837 7596
The Gardens were founded by the Royal Dublin Society in 1795 and contain some 20,000 species and varieties of trees, plants and shrubs, many housed within the elegance of Victorian curvilinear glasshouses. *Opening Times: March-Oct, Mon-Sat 9am-6pm, Sun 11am-6pm; Nov-Feb, Mon-Sat 10am-4.30pm, Sun 11am-4.30pm. Admission is free.*

NATIONAL GALLERY OF IRELAND
See page 80.

NATIONAL LIBRARY OF IRELAND
See page 81.

NATIONAL MUSEUM OF IRELAND
See page 81.

NATIONAL TRANSPORT MUSEUM
See page 81.

NATIONAL WAX MUSEUM
See page 81.

NATURAL HISTORY MUSEUM
See page 81.

NEWBRIDGE HOUSE
Donabate, County Dublin (See page 65)
Phone 843 6534
The house is actually a large mansion, built for the Archbishop of Dublin in 1737. It stands in 350 acres of park land and boasts one of the finest Georgian interiors in Ireland. There is much of interest outside the house as well, including a dairy, a forge and a traditional farm with farmyard animals. *Opening Times: April-Sept, Tues-Sat 10am-5pm, Sun 2pm-6pm; Oct-March, Sat & Sun 2pm-5pm. Admission charge is £2.95 per adult.*

NEWMAN HOUSE `25 H8`
85-86 St Stephen's Green
Phone 706 7422
Cardinal Newman founded a Catholic University here in the mid-19th century and former scholars include the poet Gerard Manley Hopkins and James Joyce. The building has some of the finest Georgian interiors to be seen anywhere in Dublin. *Opening Times: June-Aug, Tues-Fri 12noon-5pm, Sat 2pm-5pm, Sun 11am-2pm.*

NUMBER TWENTY NINE
See page 81.

OLD JAMESON DISTILLERY `24 F7`
Bow Street, Dublin 7
Phone 807 2355
The Old Jameson Distillery illustrates the ancient craft of whiskey making with the help of an audio-visual presentation, a museum and, of course, the Jameson bar where you can sample a drop or two of the 'water of life'. *Opening Times: Mon-Sun 9.30am-6pm (last tour 5pm). Admission charge is £3.50 per adult.*

THE PHOENIX PARK `23 D7`
The Phoenix Park is the largest city park in Europe, covering 1760 acres and surrounded by a wall which is 8 miles long. The park is predominantly open grassland, grazed by a herd of deer, but it has a few notable

The National Gallery of Ireland

residents including the Irish President who lives at Aras an Uachtaráin . The main visitor attraction is Dublin Zoo (see page 75) but another place of interest is the Phoenix Park Visitor Centre which is in the grounds of the old Papal Nunciature near to the Phoenix monument. The main entrance to the park is on Parkgate Street.

ST MICHAN'S CHURCH `24 F7`
Church Street
The church houses an organ which is thought to have been played by Handel, but the main attraction is the mummified bodies which can be viewed in the crypt!

ST PATRICK'S CATHEDRAL `25 G8`
Patrick's Close
Phone 4754817
Like Christ Church, St Patrick's is a Church of Ireland cathedral with an ancient and chequered history. The current building dates back to 1191 but a church has stood on this site since 450 A.D., marking the fact that Saint Patrick used a well within the cathedral grounds to baptise converts into the Christian faith. The cathedral was ravaged by fires and storms during the 14th century and its appearance today owes much to 19th century restoration work paid for by the Guinness family. Jonathan Swift, author of Gulliver's Travels, was Dean of St Patrick's from 1713 to 1745, and he is buried within its walls. The cathedral's choir school was established in 1432 and the choir took part in the first performance of Handel's Messiah back in 1742. *Opening times: Mon-Fri 9am-6pm, Sat 9am-5pm (4pm November to March), Sun 10am-4.30pm. Admission charge is £2 per adult.*

ST STEPHEN'S GREEN `25 H8`
As soon as they glimpse the summer sun, many

Temple Bar - Dublin's answer to Paris's Left Bank

Dubliners make straight for natural delights of St Stephen's Green. This urban oasis was originally a piece of common land used for public hangings among other things but, by 1880, it had become a public garden thanks to the benevolence of Lord Ardilaun, a member of the Guinness family.

SHAW'S BIRTHPLACE `31 G9`
33 Synge St, Dublin 8
Phone 475 0854
Life for George Bernard Shaw, playwright and Nobel Prize winner, began in this Victorian terrace, and the interior has been restored to reflect life at that time. *Opening Times: May-Oct, Mon-Sat 10am-5pm, Sun 11am-5pm. Admission charge is £2.60 per adult.*

TEMPLE BAR `25 G7`
The Temple Bar area is sandwiched between Dame Street and the river, with Westmoreland Street to the east and Fishamble Street to the west acting as its other boundaries. This is one of the oldest areas of Dublin but it had been in decline for many years when plans were made in the 1980's to redevelop a large part of it as a bus station! Enter Irish Taoiseach (Prime Minister), Charles Haughey, who decided that Temple Bar should become the beneficiary of several major cultural projects. Like President Miterrand of France,

Mr Haughey hoped that his lasting legacy would be to the Arts although, as things turned out, most Dubliners remember him for the large financial gifts which he received from the retailing millionaire, Ben Dunne. Temple Bar, as it happens, is often described as Dublin's Left Bank, and this is probably a fair description. The area, which is characterised by its narrow cobbled streets, is now peppered with galleries, design studios, theatres, cinemas, cultural centres, alternative shops and many good pubs, clubs and restaurants. On the downside, the success of the area has attracted a lot of stag and hen nights, and celebrations have been known to get out of hand occasionally. Businesses have recently responded, however, and stag groups are now banned from pubs and clubs in Temple Bar.

TRINITY COLLEGE & THE BOOK OF KELLS
College Green, Dublin 2 `25 G7`
Phone 608 2320
Founded in 1592 by Queen Elizabeth I and built on land confiscated from the Priory of All Hallows, Trinity College is the oldest university in Ireland. Despite its city centre location, the 40 acre campus is a tranquil world containing an impressive array of buildings dating from the 17th to the 20th century. The college has had an uneasy relationship with the Catholic Church, and it was not until the death of Archbishop McQuaid in 1970 that the Church lifted its boycott and proclaimed that it was no longer a mortal sin for a Catholic to attend Trinity. The college displays many treasures, the best known being the Book of Kells, a 9th century illustrated manuscript of the Gospels, often described as 'the most beautiful book in the world'. Other visitor attractions include 'The Dublin Experience', a 45 minute audio-visual show which tells the story of Dublin from Viking times to present day. There is free public access to the College and it is well worth a visit just to sample the rarefied atmosphere of its cobbled squares and college greens. The Old Library is open Mon-Sat 9.30am-5pm, Sun 12noon-4.30pm. The Dublin Experience is open May-Sept, 10am-5pm. There is an admission charge of £3.50 per adult to see the Old Library which houses the Book of Kells, and £3 to view The Dublin Experience.

WHITEFRIAR STREET CHURCH `25 G8`
57 Aungier Street, Dublin 2
Phone 475 8821
The church stands on the site of a Carmelite Priory which was founded in 1278, but the current building was not started until 1825. The church contains several interesting relics donated by Pope Gregory XVI in 1835, the best known being the remains of St Valentine.

The list that follows is certainly NOT an exhaustive one - Dublin has an array of small galleries dotted around the city, especially in the Temple Bar district. The admission prices listed below are based on one adult, but concessions are normally available for children and groups, and sometimes for students and the unemployed. For more detailed information, simply phone the appropriate number given below.

CENTRAL LIBRARY   `25 G7`
Henry Street, Dublin 1
Phone 873 4333
The library, which occupies the upper floor of the ILAC Centre, is the hub of Dublin's public library system. Facilities include a useful reference section, a language centre and a video viewing room. *Opening Times: Mon-Thurs 10am-8pm; Fri-Sat 10am-5pm.*

CHESTER BEATTY LIBRARY & GALLERY OF ORIENTAL ART   `25 G7`
Dublin Castle, Dame Street
His collection of 22,000 items was bequeathed to the nation by Sir Alfred Chester Beatty in 1956 and it contains a treasure trove of Islamic manuscripts, Chinese, Japanese, Indian and other Oriental art. Biblical papyri, other early Christian manuscripts, Western prints and printed books complete one of the richest collections of its kind in the world. *Opening Times: Mon-Fri 10am-5pm, Sat & Sun 2pm-5pm.*

DUBLIN CIVIC MUSEUM   `25 G8`
58 South William Street, Dublin 2
Phone 679 4260
Dublin Civic Museum aims to improve our knowledge and understanding of Dublin, its history and its people. Exhibits range from a collection of objects from Viking Dublin to the head from a statue of Lord Nelson which used to stand in O'Connell Street until it was blown up by the IRA in1966! *Opening Times: Tues-Sat 10am-6pm, Sun 11am-2pm. Admission is free.*

DUBLIN WRITERS MUSEUM   `17 G9`
18 Parnell Square North, Dublin 1
Phone 872 2077
Housed in a beautifully restored 18th century Georgian mansion, the Writers Museum opened in 1991 to mark the great literary tradition which Dublin has cultivated over the past 300 years. On display are letters, first editions, portraits and other personal items belonging to a galaxy of Irish writers including Joyce, Shaw, Beckett, Wilde, Yeats, Swift, Sheridan,

O'Casey and Behan. The museum hosts exhibitions and readings and has a special room devoted to children's literature. A special feature is Tara's Palace, a 23 room doll's house based on three great 18th century Irish mansions. *Opening Times: Mon-Sat 10am-5pm, Sun 11am-5pm. Late opening until 6pm Mon-Fri during June, July & August. Admission charge is £3 per adult.*

FRY MODEL RAILWAY MUSEUM
Malahide Castle Demesne (See page 65)
Phone 8463779
The impressive model railway layout recreates much of Ireland's transport system in miniature and is complimented by separate displays of hand crafted railway models and other memorabilia. An absolute must for train spotters! Admission price is £2.85 per adult, or £4.75 for a combined ticket which lets you see Malahide Castle while you are there. Opening times are as complicated as a railway timetable: April-Sept, Mon-Thurs/Sat 10am-5pm, Sun 2pm-6pm; Oct-Mar, Sat/Sun 2pm-5pm.

GAA MUSEUM   `17 H5`
Croke Park, Clonliffe Road, Dublin 3
Phone 836 3222
The museum charts the history of the Gaelic Athletic Association since it was founded in 1884. Displays include trophies and artefacts from the games of Gaelic Football and Hurling, with audio visual and touchscreen technology on hand to help recall famous games and players from past and present. *Opening Times: Mon-Sun 10am-5pm; closed Mondays from Oct-April. Admission charge is £3 per adult.*

THE GALLERY OF PHOTOGRAPHY   `25 G7`
Meeting House Square, Temple Bar
Phone 671 4654
Ireland's only gallery devoted exclusively to photography plays host to both Irish and international exhibitions, which are accompanied by talks and workshops. Services available include restoring and copying old photographs. *Opening Times: Mon-Sat 11am-6pm*

HERALDIC MUSEUM & GENEALOGICAL OFFICE   `25 H8`
2 Kildare Street, Dublin 2
Phone 677 7444
Coats of arms are the subject here and, for a fee, the Genealogical Office will dispense advice on how best to trace your own ancestry. *Opening Times: Mon-Fri 10am-12.30pm & 2.30pm-4.30pm. Admission is free.*

HUGH LANE MUNICIPAL GALLERY OF MODERN ART `17 G6`
Parnell Square, Dublin 1
Phone 8741903
Situated in Charlemont House, a magnificent 18th century townhouse, the gallery is named after Hugh Lane, an Irish art lover who bequeathed many major works to the gallery after his death in the 1915 sinking of the Lusitania. French Impressionists are well represented with works by Manet, Monet, Degas and Renoir, and there is also a large collection of Irish art including paintings by J B Yeats and stained glass panels by Harry Clarke. Facilities include an excellent café, and the gallery hosts free concerts on Sunday at noon between September and June. *Opening Times: Tues-Thurs 9.30am-6pm, Fri &Sat 9.30am-5pm, Sun 11am-5pm. Late opening until 8pm on Thursdays from April to August. Admission is free.*

IRISH JEWISH MUSEUM `31 G9`
3-4 Walworth Road, Dublin 8
Phone 676 0737
The museum, which is housed in a restored synagogue, chronicles the history of Jews in Ireland. *Opening Times: May-Sept, Tues/Thurs/Sun 11am-3.30pm; Oct-April, Sun 11am-3.30pm.*

IRISH MUSEUM OF MODERN ART `24 E8`
Royal Hospital, Military Road, Kilmainham
Phone 612 9900
Modelled on Les Invalides in Paris, the Royal Hospital was built in 1684, not as a hospital, but as a home for retired soldiers and it remained so until earlier this century. One of the finest buildings in Ireland, it was restored in 1986 and opened as a museum in 1991. Its permanent collection, together with temporary exhibitions, provide a showcase for Irish and international art mainly from the second half of the 20th century. *Opening Times: Tues-Sat 10am-5.30pm, Sun 12noon-5.30pm. Admission is free.*

JAMES JOYCE CENTRE `17 G6`
35 North Great George's Street, Dublin 1
Phone 878 8547
The James Joyce Centre is housed in a beautifully restored 18th century Georgian townhouse which, although associated with Joyce, was never actually his home. The centre promotes the life and work of Joyce with daily talks, conducted tours of the house, and a walking tour through the Joyce country of north Dublin. Facilities include a coffee shop and bookshop, and visitors are welcome to use the Guinness Reference Library. *Opening Times: Mon-Sat 9.30am-5pm, Sun 12.30pm-5pm. Admission is £2.75 to the* house and £6 for the house and the walking tour.

JAMES JOYCE MUSEUM
Joyce Tower, Sandycove (See page 65)
Phone 280 9265
The museum is housed in a Martello Tower where Joyce stayed for a week in 1904 as the guest of Oliver St John Gogarty who inspired Joyce to create the unsavoury character of Buck Mulligan. Much of the first chapter of Ulysses is actually set in the tower. Exhibits include letters, books, photographs and personal possessions of Joyce. *Opening Times: April-Oct, Mon-Sat 10am-5pm, Sun 2pm-6pm. Admission charge is £2.60 per adult.*

KILMAINHAM GAOL `23 D8`
Inchicore Road, Kilmainham
Phone 453 5984
The jail opened in 1796 but it has not held any prisoners since 1924. Today it is a museum to the countless Irish patriots who were imprisoned here from 1798 until the release the last inmate, Eamon de Valera, who went on to become prime minister, then president of Ireland. The darkest episode in the gaol's history was the execution of Patrick Pearse, James Connolly and 14 other leaders of the 1916 Easter Rising. A guided tour of the jail includes an audio-visual presentation and various exhibits relating to the struggle for Irish independence. *Opening Times: Apr-Sept, Mon-Sun 9.30am-4.45pm; Oct-Mar, Mon-Fri 9.30am-4pm, Sun 10am-4.45pm. Admission is £3 per adult.*

MARSH'S LIBRARY `25 G8`
St Patrick's Close, Dublin 8
Phone 454 3511
Founded in 1701 by Archbishop Narcissus Marsh and built beside St Patrick's Cathedral, Marsh's Library is the oldest public library in Ireand. It was designed by Sir William Robinson who was also the architect for the Royal Hospital, Kilmainham. The library contains 25,000 books and manuscripts, most dating from the 16th to the 18th centuries. The interior is dominated by carved oak and includes three wired alcoves or 'cages' where scholars were once locked in while they studied rare volumes. *Opening Times: Mon/Wed-Fri 10am-12.45pm & 2pm-5pm; Sat 10.30am-12.45pm. Visitors to the library are asked to donate £1.*

NATIONAL GALLERY OF IRELAND `25 H8`
Merrion Square West, Dublin 2
Phone 661 5133
The National Gallery of Ireland first opened in 1864 but by the late 1980's it had fallen on hard times, so much so that one art-lover was able to remove a small

French oil and post it back to the gallery in protest at the state of disrepair and lack of security. How times have changed. The Gallery has recently undergone major refurbishment which has allowed the number of works on show to be doubled. It now ranks among the leading state galleries in Europe, attracting over one million visitors a year to view a collection which includes work by Rembrandt, Titian, Goya, El Greco, Monet, Degas and Picasso. Further expansion is planned by the year 2000 by which time there will be a gallery within a gallery, the Jack B Yeats Museum, featuring works by the artist brother of the poet W B Yeats. There are free guided tours of the gallery at 3pm on Saturdays, and on Sundays at 2.15pm, 3pm and 4pm. *Opening Times: Mon-Sat 10am-5.30pm, Thurs 10am-8.30pm, Sun 2pm-5pm. Admission is free.*

NATIONAL LIBRARY OF IRELAND `25 H8`
Kildare Street, Dublin 2
Phone 603 0200
With over half a million volumes and an historic collection of Irish newspapers, photographs, maps and prints, this is the country's leading library for Irish studies. You will need a reader's ticket, which can be obtained free of charge, to enjoy the Reading Room with its stately dome. *Opening Times: Mon 10am-9pm; Tues-Wed 2pm-9pm; Thurs-Fri 10am-5pm; Sat 10am-1pm.*

NATIONAL MUSEUM OF IRELAND `25 H8`
Kildare Street, Dublin 2
Phone 677 7444
Opened in 1890, the National Museum contains a magnificent collection of Irish treasures and artefacts dating from the Stone Age to the 20th century. The Centrecourt houses the Or-Ireland's Gold exhibition featuring jewellery and metal work dating from the Bronze Age, 4,000 years ago. The Treasury displays the Ardagh Chalice, Tara Brooch, Cross of Cong and many other examples of outstanding medieval Celtic craftsmanship, accompanied by an audio-visual programme explaining their archaeological background. Other displays include Ancient Egypt and Viking-age Ireland. *Opening Times: Tues-Sat 10am-5.00pm, Sun 2pm-5pm. Admission is free.*

NATIONAL MUSEUM OF IRELAND `24 F7`
Collins Barracks, Benburb St, Dublin 7
Phone 677 7444
Housed in the oldest military Barracks in Europe, this is a new museum space acquired by the National Museum to house its collection of decorative arts and artefacts relating to the economic, social, political and military history of the state. Displays include silver work, ceramics, glass, period furniture, weaponry, scientific instruments and textiles. *Opening Times: Tues-Sat 10am-5pm, Sun 2pm-5pm. Admission is free.*

NATIONAL WAX MUSEUM `17 G6`
Granby Row, Parnell Square, Dublin 1
Phone 872 6340
The National Wax Museum serves up familiar offerings which include the Chamber of Horrors and the Hall of the Megastars where you can see the likes of Madonna, Elvis Presley, Michael Jackson and U2. Other features include the Children's World of Fairytale and Fantasy, and an array of famous, and not so famous, figures from Irish history. *Opening Times: Mon-Sat 10am-6pm, Sun 12noon-6pm. Admission charge is £3.50 per adult.*

NATURAL HISTORY MUSEUM `25 G8`
Merrion Street, Dublin 2
Phone 677 7444
The Natural History Museum has changed very little since Doctor Livingstone delivered the opening lecture in 1857. It houses a diverse collection of world wildlife, mainly of the stuffed variety. The ground floor is devoted largely to Irish mammals, birds, sea creatures and insects, and exhibits include the extinct giant Irish deer. The World collection is on the first floor and includes the skeletons of two humpback whales washed up on Irish shores, a giant panda and a pygmy hippopotamus. *Opening Times: Tues-Sat 10am-5pm, Sun 2pm-5pm. Admission is free.*

NATIONAL TRANSPORT MUSEUM
Howth Castle Demesne, Howth (See page 65)
Phone 847 5623
Museum run by a group of volunteers dedicated to the preservation of Ireland's transport heritage. Exhibits include old buses, trams, fire engines and military vehicles.
Opening Times: Mon-Fri 10am-5pm, Sat & Sun 2pm-5pm. Admission charge is £1.50 per adult.

NUMBER TWENTY NINE `25 H8`
29 Lower Fitzwilliam Street, Dublin 2
Phone 702 6165
Fitzwilliam Street epitomises Georgian Dublin and the idea behind number 29 is to convey what it was like, from the inside, to live here as a middle class family in the early 1800's. The house has been preserved by the Electricity Board in an act of contrition for tearing down most of the rest of the street to build an ugly 1960's office block. *Opening Times: Tues-Sat 10am-5pm, Sun 2pm-5pm. Admission charge is £2.50 per adult.*

If you are planning an evening out at the theatre, cinema or a performance of live music or comedy, it's a good idea to pick up a free copy of the Dublin Event Guide which is published fortnightly and is available in many shops, cafés and venues around the city. Alternatively, you can invest £1.95 in a copy of In Dublin magazine which is similar in format to London's Time Out. It provides an excellent and comprehensive guide to what's on, including a series of current reviews.

THEATRE

For a city steeped in literary tradition it is only fitting that the Dublin theatre scene is a vibrant one. The **Abbey** is the most famous theatre in town, premiering the work of many Irish playwrights (see below). It occupies the mainstream along with the **Gate** and the **Gaiety**, but variety abounds, with theatres such as the **Peacock**, the **Project**, the **New Theatre** and the **Focus** staging many works of a more experimental nature. And with new writing talent such as Frank McGuinness and Martin McDonagh, Irish theatre goers are able to enjoy a good selection of contemporary drama as well as the catalogue of better known work from the past.

Dublin theatre is very accessible and need not be expensive. The dramatic societies of **Trinity College** and **UCD** may be amateur companies but their output is often of a high standard. Both societies perform two plays a week from October through to April, one at lunchtime and one in the evening. The prices are very cheap and Trinity Players Theatre is especially convenient to the city centre. Some pubs, most notably the Dame Tavern and the International, also stage live performances which can offer a lot of entertainment for just a few pounds.

The highlight of the theatrical calendar is the **Dublin Theatre Festival** and its **Fringe**. The main festival runs for two weeks in mid-October, while the fringe starts a week earlier and runs for three weeks. The theatre festival has been running for longer than the Edinburgh Festival and, like its Scottish counterpart, it manages to attract performers from the four corners of the globe. The festival programme is available from late August and booking begins three weeks before opening. For more information, visit the web site on http:/www.iftn.ie/dublinfestival or telephone 677 8439. The fringe festival focuses primarily on the lighter side of life and includes a wide variety of comedy, cabaret, dance and musical performances, staged at a multitude of smaller venues across the city, including many pubs.

Finally, when booking theatre tickets over the phone, it might be useful to refer to the seating plans published in the theatre section of the *Golden Pages* telephone directory.

ABBEY THEATRE `25 G7`
26 Lower Abbey Street, Dublin 1
Phone 878 7222
The Abbey and the Peacock, which shares the same site, are the two theatres of the National Theatre Society which was founded in 1904 by W. B. Yeats and Lady Gregory. The original theatre was destroyed by fire in 1951 which explains the rather uninspiring 1960's replacement. One of the aims of the Society is to promote new Irish writing and, to this end, it has premiered the work of every leading Irish playwright this century including O'Casey, Synge and Friel. The acting tradition of the Abbey is no less illustrious and the Society has produced many renowned actors such as Barry Fitzgerald, Ray McAnally and Cyril Cusack. The theatre has deservedly earned an international reputation for the quality of its productions which also include the work of playwrights from beyond Irish shores.

ANDREW'S LANE THEATRE
9-13 Andrew's Lane, Dublin 2. Phone 679 5720

CITY ARTS CENTRE `25 H7`
Moss Street, Dublin 1. Phone 677 0643

CRYPT THEATRE `25 G7`
Dublin Castle, Dame Street, Dublin 2.
Phone 671 3387

DAME TAVERN `25 G8`
18 Dame Court, Dublin 2. Phone 679 3426

FOCUS THEATRE `31 H9`
6 Pembroke Place, Dublin 2. Phone 660 7109

GAIETY THEATRE `25 G8`
South King Street, Dublin 2. Phone 677 1717

GATE THEATRE `17 G6`
1 Cavendish Row, Dublin 2. Phone 874 4045

LAMBERT PUPPET THEATRE `40 Q13`
5 Clifton Lane, Monkstown . Phone 280 0974

NEW THEATRE `25 G7`
43 East Essex Street, Temple Bar. Phone 670 3361

OLYMPIA THEATRE `25 G7`
72 Dame Street, Dublin 2. Phone 677 7744

PEACOCK THEATRE `25 G7`
Lower Abbey Street, Dublin 1. Phone 878 7222

PROJECT @ THE MINT `25 G7`
Henry Place. Phone 671 2321

TIVOLI THEATRE `24 F8`
135-138 Francis Street Dublin 8. Phone 454 4472

TRINITY PLAYER'S THEATRE `25 G7`
Samuel Beckett Centre, Trinity College,
College Green. Phone 608 1239

UCD DRAMA SOCIETY `38 K12`
Belfield, Dublin 4. Phone 706 8545

O'Donoghue's - home of the eternal session

MUSIC

Music is very close to Irish hearts and souls and it is almost impossible to visit Dublin without experiencing a musical encounter of one sort or another. From the buskers of Grafton Street and Temple Bar to the pubs and concert halls, there is always somebody close at hand, eager to play a tune or two.

Traditional Irish music remains very popular with locals and visitors alike, and a multitude of pubs have live sessions on a regular basis. Ireland also has a strange love affair with country & western music, but it is in the field of rock and popular music that the Irish have made their presence felt on the world stage in recent years with bands such as U2 the Cranberries, Boyzone and the Corrs, and individuals such as Van Morrison, Bob Geldof, Sinéad O'Connor and Enya, to name but a few.

Dublin is a regular tour stop for these and a host of international recording artists. Most of the big acts play at the **Point**, but large concerts also take place occasionally at Dublin's three major outdoor sporting arenas, Lansdowne Road, Croke Park and the RDS. There are quite a few good mid-sized venues which include the **Olympia Theatre**, the **Mean Fiddler, Whelan's** and the **Red Box**. The HMV music stores on Grafton Street and Henry Street are good places buy tickets in advance of the show. On a day to day basis, however, Dublin pubs and clubs provide the venues and cater to all musical persuasions, including rock, country, jazz and traditional. For more details, see pages 89-98.

For lovers of classical music, the main venue is the **National Concert Hall** which is home to the **National Symphony Orchestra** which plays most Friday evenings. Other performers, both amateurs and touring professionals, take to the stage in the main auditorium throughout the rest of the week. A wide variety of smaller concerts and lunchtime recitals takes place in the adjoining **John Field Room** which doubles up as the Concert Hall's bar area.

Other venues for classical music include the Hugh Lane Gallery, the National Gallery of Ireland and the Bank of Ireland Arts Centre. If you can't get hold of a free copy of The Event Guide, the "What's On Today" column in the Irish Times is a good place to track down performances. If you prefer the great outdoors, Dublin Corporation sponsor free Music in the Parks on Sunday afternoons during the summer months. Details of forthcoming events are available on the noticeboard in St Stephen's Green.

Dublin, unfortunately, does not have an opera house but **Opera Ireland** perform two short seasons every spring and autumn at the **Gaiety Theatre**. Rather ironically, the operatic highlight of the year is the **Wexford Festival Opera**, which takes place during the last two weeks of October. If you prefer church music, choral concerts and organ recitals are a regular feature at both St Patrick's and Christ Church Cathedrals.

NATIONAL CONCERT HALL `31 H9`
Earlsfort Terrace. Phone 475 1572

OLYMPIA THEATRE `25 G7`
74 Dame Street, Dublin 2. Phone 677 7744

POINT THEATRE `26 J7`
North Wall Quay, Dublin 1.Phone 836 3633

CINEMA

With the help of tax incentives provided by the government, the Irish film industry continues to go from strength to strength, with many notable successes such as The Commitments, Brave Heart and Saving Private Ryan. Cinema attendances have soared in recent years and the Irish now go to the 'flicks' more often than anybody else in Europe. The number of screens in and around the city continues to rise and each new multiplex seems to be followed swiftly by another one. In terms of innovation, the most interesting latecomer is the **Imax** cinema on Parnell Street where the screen is so big that you feel as if you are *in* the film, rather than just watching it.

Cinema HQ is the **Irish Film Centre** on Eustace Street which opened in 1992 and is the main outlet for foreign language and arthouse films, although the **Screen** also does its bit to break the Hollywood monopoly. The IFC is technically a members only club for over-18's, but the reality is that you simply pay a pound to be a member for a week, or £10 for annual membership. Members are then entitled to buy tickets for up to three guests. Its club status means that uncertified films are occasionally screened as the IFC does not have to submit all of its films to the censor.

The highlight of the cinematic year is the **Dublin Film Festival** which runs for a week from the beginning of March and screens an interesting mix of both Irish and international movies along with classics from the past. For more information, phone 679 2937 or e-mail dff@iol.ie. The **French Film Festival** is held in the first week of November and most screenings are at the Irish Film Centre. Phone 677 8788 for information.

And finally, a couple of tips regarding cost. As a general rule, if you want to save a few bob, go to the cinema in the afternoon and you will get in for just over half the price that it costs in the evening. If you are totally skint, *free* films are screened outdoors on Saturday nights during July and August in Meeting House Square in Temple Bar. Each film is chosen by an invited celeb who addresses the audience before the film begins. Tickets are available at the Temple Bar Information Centre on Eustace Street. Phone 671 5717.

AMBASSADOR　`25 G7`
O'Connell Street, D1. Phone 872 7000. 1 screen

CLASSIC　`30 F10`
Harold's Cross Road, D6. Phone 492 3699. 2 screens

FORUM　`41 S13`
Dun Laoghaire. Phone 280 9574

IMAX CINEMA　`25 G7`
Parnell Street, Dublin 1. Phone 817 4222

IRISH FILM CENTRE　`25 G7`
6 Eustace Street, Temple Bar. Phone 679 3477
2 screens

ORMONDE　`38 L14`
Upper Kilmacud Road, Stillorgan. Phone 278 0000
6 screens

SANTRY OMNIPLEX　`7 H2`
Santry, Dublin 9.Phone 842 8844. 10 screens

SAVOY　`25 G7`
Upper O'Connell Street, Dublin 1. Phone 874 6000
5 screens

SCREEN　`25 H7`
D'Olier Street, Dublin 2. Phone 671 4988. 3 screens

UCI MULTIPLEX
The Square, Tallaght. Phone 452 2611. 12 screens

STELLA　`31 G10`
207 Lower Rathmines Road, Dublin 6.
Phone 497 1281. 2 screens

UCI COOLOCK　`9 M2`
Malahide Road, Dublin 17. Phone 848 5122
10 screens

VIRGIN CINEMAS　`25 G7`
Parnell Street, Dublin 1. Phone 872 8444. 9 screens

COMEDY

Ireland has produced a rich crop of stand-up comedians in recent years including Ardal O'Hanlon, Sean Hughes, Dylan Moran, Ed Byrne, and Tommy Tiernan, the most recent of several Irish winners of the prestigious Perrier Award at the Edinburgh Festival. It has to be said that most of these acts were actually blooded on the London comedy circuit, but Dublin does have a few good venues of its own which are helping to keep the production line rolling.

The most established venue is the Comedy Cellar which is upstairs at the **International Bar** on Wicklow Street (phone 677 9250). Wednesday and Thursday are the main nights for stand-up, Mondays for improv, and there are open mike spots for anybody who wants to make a total eedjit of themselves. Other pub venues include the **Norseman** on East Essex Street (phone 677 9250) and the **Ha'penny Bridge Inn** on Wellington Quay (phone 677 0616), the latter staging weekly shows on both Tuesday and Thursday nights. You can combine comedy with pizza on a Sunday night at **Milano's** on Dawson Street (670 7744), and there are regular performances by big name comedians at **Murphy's Laughter Lounge** on Eden Quay (phone 874 4611).

ANGLING

There is fresh water fishing on certain stretches of the River Liffey for salmon, trout, pike and perch. The River Tolka is also popular with trout fishermen and there is some coarse fishing on Dublin's two canals. Fishing permits are available from tackle shops. Howth and Dun Laoghaire are the main centres for sea fishing.

BOWLING

There are several ten pin bowling alleys in and around Dublin, many of which are open 24 hours a day. Stillorgan has the oldest bowling alley in Ireland and it hosts all the major competitions including the Irish Open. Prices depend on the day and time, but the cheapest period is usually before 6pm on weekdays. A couple of the more centrally located alleys are listed below:

Leisureplex   `39 M14`
Stillorgan. Phone 288 1656

Leisureplex   `9 M2`
Malahide Road, Coolock, Dublin 17. Phone 848 5722

Outdoor bowling greens are in short supply in Dublin, but there's one in Moran Park in Dun Laoghaire and another, which is closer to the centre of town, in Herbert Park in Ballsbridge.

CYCLING

There is a strong cycling tradition in Ireland which was recently recognised when the 1998 Tour de France held its first stage in Dublin to honour the international success of Sean Kelly and Stephen Roche. The biggest domestic event is the FBD Milk Race which takes place during the last two weeks of May, starting and finishing in Dublin.

There are no indoor cycling arenas in the city but there is an outdoor track in the Eamonn Ceannt Park in Crumlin which is open to the public. Phone 679 6111. If you simply want to hire a bike and do a bit of exploring, there are several bike hire shops in and around the city. See page 69.

GAELIC GAMES

Gaelic football and hurling are Ireland's two national sports, and both have their headquarters at Croke Park which is Ireland's finest sports stadium (phone 836 3222). Both games retain their amateur status and are governed by the Gaelic Athletic Association (GAA) which was founded in 1884 to promote indigenous games. In doing so, its aim was to forge a distinctive Irish identity during a period of British rule in Ireland.

Gaelic football is a fast and physical game, often likened to Australian Rules football which itself evolved from Irish roots, although the Irish play with a round ball. Ireland's 32 counties compete for a place in the All Ireland Final which takes place at Croke Park on the third Sunday

in September in front of 80,000 spectators. Tickets for the final are very hard to come by but a trip to one of the earlier rounds at Croke Park will provide a flavour of the event. Parnell Park in Donnycarney is a good place to catch big club games which generally take place on Saturday evenings during the summer months and Sunday afternoons during the winter (phone 851 0650). The All Ireland club finals take place at Croke Park on 17th March, St Patrick's Day.

Hurling is played with a stick and a ball and is a game of great skill and co-ordination, despite taking on the appearance of open warfare at times. The All Ireland hurling final is staged on the first Sunday in September, also at Croke Park. Dublin may be a force to be reckoned with at football, but the hurling final is usually contested by teams from out of town.

GOLF

Unlike the situation in many other counties, golf is not an elitist game in Ireland. Many of the world's finest courses are close to hand but there are many alternatives to suit players of all abilities, and green fees tend not to be prohibitively expensive. Royal Dublin and Portmarnock are two Dublin courses of international renown, and other fine courses in and around the city include Castle, Grange, Hermitage, Island, Malahide, Milltown and Woodbrook. These clubs are all private but visitors are welcome, especially during the week. Municipal courses offer a cheaper alternative, and there are a number of par-3 and pitch and putt courses dotted around the city. If you want to see how the game really should be played, take a trip to the Irish Open which is one of the leading tournaments on the European Tour, attracting many of the world's top players. The venue changes, as does the timing, but the event is normally staged in early July.

GREYHOUND RACING

Greyhound racing is very popular in Ireland, and there are two venues in Dublin. Meetings are staged all year round at Shelbourne Park Stadium on South Lotts Road on Mondays, Wednesdays and Saturdays at 8pm (phone 668 3502); and at Harold's Cross Stadium on Harold's Cross Road on Tuesdays, Thursdays and Fridays at 8pm (phone 497 1081) .

HORSE RACING & RIDING

Ireland is famous around the globe for breeding and training some of the world's greatest thoroughbreds (and it produces a few good horses into the bargain!). Many Dubliners enjoy a flutter on the horses and the most convenient place for them to be parted from their cash is Leopardstown Race Course which is only a few miles from the city centre in the suburb of Foxrock. The annual highlight is the Hennessy Cognac Gold Cup which takes place in February.

The Irish Grand National is run on Easter Monday at

Fairyhouse which is about 15 miles north of the city. The headquarters of Irish flat racing is 30 miles south west of Dublin at the Curragh which hosts all five Classics, including the Irish Derby which is a major social occasion. Other courses within an hour's drive of Dublin include Naas and Punchestown which are both in County Kildare. All national newspapers carry details of the day's race meetings and special buses run from Busarus on race days.

Away from the track, the RDS (Royal Dublin Society) hosts the Dublin Horse Show each year in August. This is a major international show jumping event which attracts hundreds of competitors from around the world and thousands of spectators. If you prefer riding them to betting on them, there are many riding centres in and round Dublin including Brennanstown Riding School near Bray which offers cross-country rides in the scenic Wicklow Hills (phone 286 3778).

KARTING

Budding Formula One drivers of all ages can hone their skills on three indoor circuits. Advanced booking is recommended as karting has become a very popular corporate jaunt, and the circuits are sometimes entirely booked up for the event.

Kart City   `7 H2`
Santry, Dublin 9. Phone 842 6322

Kylemore Karting Centre   `28 A10`
Killeen Road, Dublin 10. Phone 626 1444

Phibsboro Karting Centre   `17 G5`
Prospect Road, Dublin 7. Phone 830 8777

RUGBY

The Lansdowne Road stadium in Ballsbridge is the headquarters of the Irish Rugby Football Union - phone 668 4601. The highlight of the year is the Six Nations Championship which takes place from January to March when Ireland take on England, Scotland, Wales, France and Italy. Despite a conspicuous lack of Irish success on the field, tickets are very difficult to acquire, and the thousands of foreign invaders help to turn these matches into a great social occasion.

SKATING & SKIING

Ireland may not be renowned for its achievements in the Winter Olympics but it's possible to go ice skating in the city, either at the Dublin Ice Rink on South Circular Road in Dolphin's Barn (phone 453 4153) or at the Silver Skate Ice Rink on North Circular Road, Dublin 7 (phone 830 4405). Skiers can practise their falls on the artificial ski slope in Kilternan which is open to the public from September through to March (phone 295 5658).

SNOOKER

There are quite a few snooker halls in and around the city, the most famous of which is Jason's of Ranelagh, home to Ken Doherty, the world champion in 1997. A full list of clubs and halls can be found in the Golden Pages.

SOCCER

For many years Irish soccer lived in the shadow of Gaelic games until big Jack (Charlton) came from England, of all places, to manage the national side. Ten years of unprecedented success in the European Championships and the World Cup gripped the nation. Jack recently returned to his fishing rod and the team is currently being rebuilt by a new manager, Mick McCarthy. International matches are played at Lansdowne Road stadium but the headquarters of the Football Association of Ireland are at 80 Merrion Square - phone 676 6864.

The top three Dublin teams are St Patrick's Athletic who play in Inchicore, and Shelbourne and Shamrock Rovers who share a small stadium in Drumcondra. All three teams play in the League of Ireland, usually on Sundays, but support for local league sides is dwarfed by the passionate interest which Dubliners take in the English Premiership.

SWIMMING & WATER SPORTS

If you aren't afraid of cold water, there are beaches just outside the city at Dollymount and Malahide to the north, and Sandymount and Merrion to the south. Alternatively, the Forty Foot Pool offers a rare opportunity to immerse yourself in both the Irish Sea and Irish literature. Follow in the footsteps of Buck Mulligan who went there for a bracing dip in James Joyce's novel, Ulysses. The pool, which is named after the 40th Regiment of Foot who used to be stationed nearby, is overlooked by the Joyce Tower and is easily reached by taking the DART to Sandycove. If you aren't feeling quite so hardy, a list of indoor swimming pools can be found in the Golden Pages.

Sailing is a popular activity, especially around Howth and Dun Laoghaire, but sailing clubs are usually restricted to members only. The Irish National Sailing School, however, offers courses for all levels throughout the year. The school is situated by Dun Laoghaire's West Pier - phone 284 4195. Wind surfing is another popular activity in this area of town and equipment and tuition are available from Wind & Wave Water Sports in Monkstown (phone 284 4177).

TENNIS

Since most tennis clubs are privately run for the benefit of members and their guests, the most realistic option is a game in one of the city's parks. There are public courts at Bushy Park in Terenure (phone 490 0320), Herbert Park in Ballsbridge (phone 668 4364) and in St Anne's Park in Raheny (833 1859).

Dublin shops generally open Monday to Saturday from 9am to 6pm, with late shopping in the city centre on Thursday until 8pm. Some city centre department stores and book shops open on Sunday, usually from 12 noon until 6pm. Visitors from outside the European Community can claim a rebate on the purchase price of items carrying Value Added Tax. Inquire at the time of purchase for more details.

FASHION

The English high street invasion has lobotomised much of Dublin's shopping experience, but Irish flair and ambience remains in abundance. Busker-friendly Grafton Street is central to any retail therapy, and the total shopping extravaganza that is **Brown Thomas** department store is usually the first stop for any self respecting platinum card holder. The store is filled with five star luxury, but without the snobbishness which is prevalent in similar emporiums elsewhere.

Further up Grafton Street, the Brown Thomas moniker has been shortened to **BT2** to catch those who find street life unbearable without a Prada jacket, Helmut Lang jeans, DKNY sweatshirt or Ralph's pony. Cash-strapped wannabees should make their way to the BT owned **A-wear**. Don't be put off by the uninspiring exterior, for there are treasures to be found within, especially in the designer section where Quinn and Donnelly rule supreme.

Grafton Street - Dublin's College of Retail Therapy

Bypassing **Wallis, River Island, Miss Selfridge, Jigsaw, Vero Moda,** and **Monsoon,** brings you to **Dunnes Stores.** Its St Bernard brand is not as reliable as its multinational competitor, **Marks and Spencer,** but there are often very good quality outfits on offer at considerably less cost, and it is certainly worth checking out one of the many branches around Dublin. The Grafton Street store looks classier but their outlet in St Stephen's Green Shopping Centre has more content.

On the way there, thirty somethings might like to flex their flexible friends in **Airwave,** which stocks In Wear, Matinique, and similar labels for both men and women. Ladies of a certain age will enjoy the classic look with a twist at **Pia Bang,** and the sheer classic look at **Richard Allen.** Foot fetishists can satisfy their desires at elegant **Carl Scarpa,** eclectic **Zerep** and downright tub-thumping **Korky.**

Behind the wrought iron and glass facade of **St Stephen's Green Shopping Centre,** it is worth checking out **Sasha, Waterhammer** and **Envy,** among others. Right at the other end of Grafton Street, on Suffolk Street, **Makulla's** is a clubber's Mecca, and look out for branches of **Hobo** if you are into boho. Nassau Street is home to several Oirish shops but don't turn back until you have reached the **Kilkenny Design Centre.** Whereas their stock in trade used to focus on lumpy tweed suits and itchy Aran sweaters which appealed mainly to garishly dressed Americans attempting to return to their roots, the new order epitomises the slick marketing of 1990's Ireland, with a splendid self service restaurant, designer clothing and a range of ceramics and knick knacks which would be at home on the style pages of a Sunday magazine.

Back on Grafton Street, for men, **F X Kelly** and **Club Tricot** will turn you out in designer European labels, but at a price, as will **Alias Tom** on Duke Lane. **Royal Hibernian Way,** which runs west from Grafton Street to Dawson Street, has a modern collection of sleek and shiny shops and boutiques. East, off Grafton Street, is **Westbury Mall** which leads to **Whistles** on **Balfe St.** Don't worry, however, if you are not a size 8, six foot tall model since the staff, typical of Dublin, are friendly, chatty, relaxed and non-judgmental.

Behind the Westbury is **Powerscourt Townhouse,** a beautifully converted Georgian mansion and courtyard, housing crafts, jewellery, clothing and furniture, as well as some excellent eating houses to stave off the munchies. **The Design Centre,** on the first floor, features many of Ireland's most talented clothes designers all of whom manage to combine excellent tailoring, quality fabrics and elegance with a bearable price tag.

Behind Powerscourt, down narrow streets are more Bohemian markets and shops leading onto Great George's Street and Aungier Street. This is an area to watch for the future but, where Bohemia is concerned, Temple Bar still leads the way, although the area will no doubt be invaded by more upmarket designer boutiques. At present, however, it is still home to second hand shops, record stores, and the cheaper more 'hippy' look that impoverished Irish students favour. A more hip look is also catered for by the likes of **DV8** on Crown Alley which will kit you out in some very funky footwear.

Across the Halfpenny Bridge and en route to pedestrianised Henry Street, on no account call yourself a serious shopper and miss the newly refurbished **Arnott's**. Their mid price, wearable collections of John Rocha, French Connection, and Sticky Fingers will turn heads. Henry Street has fewer tourists, and money stretches a bit further than on Grafton Street. Main outlets of note are the slightly neglected **Ilac Centre**, and the new **Jervis Centre** with perennial, functional, British favourites including **Debenhams** and **BHS**. The Moore Street fruit and vegetable market is worth a visit if only to sample a bit of the local banter.

Henry Street leads out onto O'Connell Street which is not over-endowed with classy shops, but it does have **Penny's**, and **Clery's** department store.

Despite, or perhaps because of, the inexorable rise in Dublin house prices, modern furniture and concept interior design stores have recently become an integral part of the shopping experience, with outlets such as **Haus** on Crow Street, **Urbana** on Temple Bar and **Foko** on South Great George's Street.

BOOKS

Dublin lives up to its literary reputation with a rich selection of book shops, many of which open seven days a week and close later than most other shops. Dawson Street is home to two of the heavyweights, **Waterstones** and **Hodges Figgis**. Around the corner in Nassau Street is **Fred Hanna's**, another Dublin institution, much used by students from nearby Trinity College. **The Dublin Bookshop** on Grafton Street and **Hughes & Hughes** in the St Stephen's Green Shopping Centre are both well stocked and centrally located. **Easons**, with stores on O'Connell Street and throughout Ireland, sell an excellent range of books, newspapers, magazines, stationery, art materials and a variety of other goods. Second hand book shops are too numerous to mention by name but the **Winding Stair** on Ormond Quay rates a mention for the fact that you can enjoy a bite to eat and some good views of the Liffey as well as three floors of books.

IRISH CRAFTS & TEXTILES

Ireland has a long tradition of producing excellent craftware with producers such as Waterford Crystal and Belleek Pottery firmly established in markets all around the world. As mentioned earlier, the **Kilkenny Shop** on Nassau Street has modernised both its stock and its approach in recent years and now ranks as Dublin's leading outlet for Irish craftware. One side of the shop specialises in clothes - mainly woollens, tweeds and linen while the rest of the shop is dedicated to Irish glass, pottery, ceramics and metalwork. **The Blarney Woollen Mills**, also on Nassau Street, follows a similar layout while other outlets noted for their fine selection of Irish woollens are the **Sweatershop** on Wicklow Street and **Dublin Woollen Mills** on Lower Ormond Quay.

The **Crafts Council Gallery** in the Powerscourt Townhouse displays and sells a wide range of crafts by Irish and international designers, and the **Tower Design Centre** on Pearse Street houses a number of studios for craft workers, producing jewellery, ceramics, fabrics, and other hand-crafted items. If your interest is Irish antiques, your first stop should be **Francis Street** in the Liberties area which provides ample opportunity to browse.

MUSIC

Dublin may be the city of a thousand bands but musical retailing is dominated by British superstores. **Virgin** have one of their Megastores on Aston Quay, and **HMV** have branches on Grafton Street and Henry Street. **Golden Discs**, an Irish chain, have several branches around the city. The Temple Bar area offers some welcome relief from the big players with a growing number of small independent music retailers, many catering to specific tastes. **Claddagh Records** on Cecilia Street, for example, is famous for its collection of Irish traditional and folk music.

MARKETS

The famous **Moore Street Market**, referred to earlier, operates from Monday to Saturday and specialises in fruit, vegetables and flowers. Across the river, the **Temple Bar Food Market** is held every Saturday in Meeting House Square and appeals more to the stuffed olive brigade with an impressive array of speciality foods on offer. If you are seeking shelter, there is plenty of variety on offer in the covered market in **George's Arcade**, between South Great George's Street and Drury Street. **Mother Redcap's Market** operates on Back Lane near Christ Church Cathedral from Friday to Sunday selling anything and everything from antiques to books and records. Further out of town, **Blackrock** hosts a large market every Sunday which attracts a good crowd to its diverse range of stalls.

Dublin offers many forms of entertainment, but the heart and soul of the city's social life is undoubtedly the pub. There are over a thousand to choose from, and their unique appeal owes much to the wide cross-section of customers which they attract.

Many Dublin pubs have changed very little over the past 100 years, and many more have tried to recapture the past, but an increasing number are beginning to look to the future with a strong European influence taking hold around the city. Dublin is arguably the best city in the world for pubs but the primary reason for their allure is the people who work and drink there.

Dubliners have few peers when it comes to the art of conversation, exercising a ready wit and an insatiable appetite for banter, debate and gossip. The *craic* can be mighty, and strangers can quickly become a friend.

The selection of pubs, clubs and bars below tries to point you in the direction of some of Dublin's finest watering holes but, if you feel strongly that any have been wrongly included or unfairly omitted, feel free to let us know. Most of the pubs listed serve food, and many stage live music. To find out who is playing where, pick up a copy of **The Event Guide**, a free paper published every two weeks and available in many shops, cafés and music venues. Alternatively, invest £1.95 in a copy of **In Dublin** which is similar in nature to London's Time Out, and an excellent source of up to date information.

The list below is NOT broken into categories as so many of Dublin's bars and clubs fall into more than one bracket. Many bars have a nightclub downstairs so that you can carry on drinking until late. When it comes to serious clubbing, however, the three heavyweights are the **PoD** & the **Red Box**, the **Kitchen** and **Rí-Rá** (see listings).

Opening hours have been omitted as they are often subject to extensions which can vary according to what's on. Pubs normally open their doors at 10.30am from Monday to Saturday, and at 12.30pm on Sunday. Doors are closed from 2pm-4pm on Sundays, but you will often be able to stay on during these hours as long as you are in before 2pm. Closing time is 11.30 pm from May until September, and 11pm in winter and on Sundays. Half an hour drinking up time is allowed after closing.

When it comes to drinking up, Guinness reigns supreme in Dublin. Brewed at St James's Gate, many Dubliners spend much of their life in search of the perfect pint. Where the Japanese have their tea ceremony, Irish barmen perform their own ritual when pouring a pint of the black stuff but, like all good things in life, it is usually worth waiting for. Competition is increasingly at hand in the form of Beamish and Murphys which are both brewed in Cork but, if you prefer a pint of ale or lager, Smithwicks and Harp dominate the market, both brewed by none other than Guinness!

The Temple Bar area has the highest concentration of pubs in the city and it tends to act as a honey pot for tourists, many of whom seem to be enjoying their last hours of freedom, although stag and hen parties have recently been banned by many Temple Bar establishments. If things are getting a bit tired and emotional', however, you need only walk a couple of hundred yards to escape the street party. City centre pubs are busy most nights of the week and so, if you are looking for a quiet drink, a hotel bar is often a good bet. Bear in mind, however, that there is no such thing as a quiet drink in Dublin come Friday and Saturday night.

Finally, if you like to keep on the move but aren't sure where you are going, there are some well organised pub crawls. The **Jameson Dublin Literary Pub Crawl** is conducted by professional actors who will bring you to a selection of Dublin's best known literary pubs, and enlighten you with performances from the works of Joyce, Beckett and Behan, among many others. The evening kicks off from The Duke on Duke Street at 7.30pm every night from Easter until the end of October, on Thursday, Friday and Saturday during the rest of year, and at 12noon on Sundays all year round. If you prefer music to literature, a **Musical Pub Crawl** starts at 7.30 pm every night, except for Fridays, from May to October at Oliver St John Gogarty's on Fleet Street. The winter schedule is limited to Friday and Saturday nights only.

If you would rather organise your own pub crawl, then feel free to work your way through the list below!

THE AULD DUBLINER   `25 G7`
17 Anglesea Street, Temple Bar
Phone 677 0527
If you are wary of salty sea-dogs who stand outside pubs, don't worry - this one is only a mural! The Auld Dub is set very much in the traditional mould but its location in the heart of Temple Bar means that a good mixture of locals and visitors make up the throng. Live traditional music on a regular basis.

BAD BOB'S BACKSTAGE BAR   `25 G7`
34 East Essex Street, Temple Bar
Phone 677 5482
Ireland has a strange love affair with country music but Bad Bob's is as close as you'll get to the 'grand old opree'. You can stand by your man on three floors - downstairs provides a venue for live music, and there's another bar and a disco upstairs.Late bar until 2.30am.

THE BAGGOT INN `25 H8`
143 Lower Baggot Street, Dublin 2
Phone 676 1430
This is Big Jack's place. If you are unfamiliar with Irish football, Jack Charlton used to be the national team manager who achieved the status of living saint while his team enjoyed a successful run lasting almost 10 years. In the style of Victor Kiam, Jack liked this pub so much he bought it, and installed his son, John, to run it. As well as being a footballing Mecca, this is one of Dublin's main venues for live rock - David Bowie chose the Baggot Inn for an unannounced gig back in 1992, and U2 and Bob Geldof performed here on a regular basis before making it big. Jazz, funk and traditional music are also on offer.

THE BAILEY
2-3 Duke Street
Dublin 2
Located just off Grafton Street, the Bailey has an unrivalled literary tradition which stretches back to the mid-19th century. Former patrons include Joyce, Yeats, and Behan, as well as Michael Collins, the evasive IRA General, who drank upstairs while on the run from the British military who were drinking downstairs! The pub no longer trades off these associations, however. Following the redevelopment of Marks & Spencers next door, the refurbished Bailey has dispensed with the literary memorabilia and opted instead for a chic interior which evokes modern Japan more than 19th century Dublin. The clientele are smart and cosmopolitan, and include plenty of Dubliners who like to recover here after a hard day at the office.

THE BARGE `31 G9`
Adelaide Road, Dublin 2
Situated on the banks of the Grand Canal, the Barge is not a boat, but a large two storey bar, expensively fitted out to achieve a traditional look of bare brick walls, wooden floors and moulded ceilings. The finished product is attractive enough to make it a popular watering hole with residents, office workers and hotel guests who tend to populate this up-market area of town. Late bar.

THE BLEEDING HORSE `31 G9`
24 Upper Camden Street, Dublin 2
Phone 475 2705
There has been a pub here since the days of Oliver Cromwell but the current building dates back only to the last century, although the exposed timbers, high ceilings, and the minstrel gallery can conjure up the image of a medieval banqueting hall after a few pints. The pub is popular with nearby office workers, and a large crowd usually takes advantage of the late night bar every Thursday, Friday and Saturday.

B L O O M S HOTEL
Anglesea Street, Temple Bar
Phone 671 5622
Blooms is a modern hotel which will not win any prizes for its architecture, but its bar and nightclub, **Club M**, are both popular with locals as well as hotel guests.

THE BRAZEN HEAD `24 F7`
20 Lower Bridge Street, Dublin 8
Phone 679 5186
Located at the end of a cobbled courtyard across the river from the Four Courts, the Brazen Head enjoys the accolade of being Dublin's oldest pub, although its exact age is a matter of some dispute. The pub sign claims the year 1198 but this actually relates to an ear-

lier tavern which used to occupy the same site. A labyrinth of low-ceilinged, smoke-filled rooms makes up the current building which is thought to date back to the early eighteenth century. The United Irishmen, led by Wolfe Tone, used to meet here, and the food is even given a mention by Joyce in *Ulysses* (his recommendation still applies today judging by the busy lunchtime trade). Regular sessions of traditional music help to pull the crowds in after dark.

BREAK FOR THE BORDER `25 G8`
Johnson Place, Dublin 2
Phone 478 0300
Break for the Border is a successful combination of bar, Tex-Mex restaurant and nightclub, laid out on three inter-connecting floors with a Western theme very much to the fore. Late drinking and music are on offer every night of the week with live performances by rock and country bands each night from Wednesday to Saturday.

THE BRIDGE `25 G7`
10 Westmoreland Street, Dublin 2
Phone 670 8133
The opening of the Bridge a few years ago marked a crossing point for Bewley's, from cafés into the world of bars and hotels. The decor is plush and comfortable and there are several themed rooms to choose from, all enjoying a late bar until 1.30am on Thursday and Friday nights. Strangely, for Dublin, this is the only pub on the street, which makes it a strategic stopping-off point close to Temple Bar. A Bewley's café and a 70 room hotel are both part of the same complex.

THE BRUXELLES `25 G8`
7 Harry Street, Dublin 2
Phone 677 5362
An impressive Victorian interior, and a few tables outside if you are hoping to catch a few rays. A prime location, just off Grafton Street, helps to keep things busy both day and night. Regular jazz sessions.

THE BURLINGTON HOTEL `31 H9`
Upper Leeson Street, Dublin 4
Phone 660 5222
One of the great things about Dublin's hotels is their lack of pretentiousness - many hotel bars are frequented by non-residents, and this is certainly the case at the Burlington. The main bar received an expensive, neo-classical face lift a few years back, and it attracts a lively crowd. The hotel caters to the tourist market with an Irish Cabaret which is staged nightly from May to October, and the hotel nightclub, **Annabel's**, remains a popular, middle of the road-type, place for

Dame Street mosaic for alert stag hunters

twenty and thirty-somethings to bop the night away.

BUSKERS `25 G7`
Fleet Street, Temple Bar
Phone 677 3333
Part of the Temple Bar Hotel, Buskers is a large, comfortable bar, laid out on a traditional shop-fronts theme. As evening approaches, a DJ is on hand to change the mood from pub to disco.

CAFE EN SEINE `25 H8`
40 Dawson Street, Dublin 2
Phone 677 4369
A continental style café bar with a beautifully designed interior which will not fail to impress. Imposing brass chandeliers hang from vaulted ceilings, the walls are decorated with large mirrors and art nouveau murals, and there's even a balcony from which to survey the congregation below. Beer, wine, spirits, and coffee enjoy a comfortable co-existence, the atmosphere is relaxed, and the background music poses no threat to the art of conversation, although the main activity seems to be people watching. The staff, decked out in their black and white uniforms, are as international as the clientele, which helps to lend a certain sophistication to the proceedings, although the recent visit of Alan Shearer and Keith Gillespie proved to be an exception to the rule. This is a great bar, and will hopefully remain so when its current expansion plans come to fruition.

THE CHOCOLATE BAR `36 D4`
Upper Hatch Street, Dublin 2
Phone 478 0166
A trend setter in its day but beginning to fray slightly at the edges. The interior is inspired by Gaudi with lighting so low that the cocktail menu should be written in Braille. Still a comfortable spot to relax with the help of a chocolate vodka and a bit of soul music

before heading next door to the POD (see below). The style statement even extends to the gents' loo which conjures up images of the Trevi Fountain. Be warned - carry a shower cap just to be on the safe side!

THE CLARENCE HOTEL `25 G7`
East Essex Street, Temple Bar
Phone 670 9000
The Clarence Hotel receives endless free publicity by virtue of the fact that it's owned by the Dublin rock band, U2. The building has undergone major refurbishment since the band took over, but their investment seems to have paid handsome dividends with the **Octagon Bar** and the **Kitchen Nightclub** firmly established among the trendiest places in town. The hotel can feel a bit exclusive, with its wood-panelled Octagon Bar catering mainly to a dry martini crowd, but the Kitchen, which is in a crypt-like vault underneath the hotel, is a late-night venue with sufficient attitude to make it one of the city's top attractions for serious clubbers.

THE DA CLUB `25 G8`
2 Johnson Place, Dublin 2
Phone 670 3137
Few frills, but a diverse mix of live music, cabaret and DJ's more than compensates. A fun night out is usually guaranteed.

DANGER DOYLE'S `25 G7`
24 Eustace Street, Temple Bar
Phone 670 6755
Deceptively large bar stretching all the way back to a rear entrance on Temple Lane. At first sight, the decor looks traditional with lots of carved wood and quarry stone floors, but closer inspection reveals a series of abstract metal sculptures which seem to owe much to a job lot of parts from a disused power station! The revelry continues downstairs until late at the **Za-Zu** nightclub.

DAVY BYRNE'S `25 G8`
21 Duke Street, Dublin 2
James Joyce immortalised a few Dublin pubs in his time and, yes, this is another one. Described, in *Ulysses*, as a moral pub, it has has undergone considerable change since it opened in 1873 - physically, rather than morally, of course. There are now three bars, all refurbished to reflect more modern times, but still retaining a few connections with the past. Davy Byrne, who ran the bar for more than 50 years, appears in one of the murals which were painted by Brendan Behan's father-in-law, no less! The pub's central location, just off Grafton Street, helps to keep it popular with businessmen, shoppers and tourists alike.

DOCKERS `26 J7`
5 Sir John Rogersons Quay, Dublin 2
Phone 677 1692
A bit off the beaten track, this is a dockside pub, frequented by U2 fans in the vain hope of bumping into Bono and the boys. The band recorded their early albums at the Windmill Studios which used to be just around the corner.

DOHENY & NESBITT `25 H8`
5 Lower Baggot Street, Dublin 2
Phone 676 2945
Much unimproved! - Nesbitts is very much the genuine article when it comes to an early Victorian pub, right down to the bare floor boards, smoke stained ceilings, and a bar complete with wooden partitions. Situated around the corner from the Irish Parliament, this is a favourite watering hole for lawyers, politicians and the press pack. Traditional music sessions are a regular feature.

THE DUKE `25 G8`
9 Duke Street, Dublin 2
Phone 679 9553
Characterful pub, just off Grafton Street, and starting point for the Literary Pub Crawl (see page 89).

EAMONN DORAN'S `25 G7`
3A Crown Alley, Temple Bar
Phone 679 9114
Upstairs is a busy, New York-style bar cum restaurant where you can listen to live Irish traditional music several nights a week. Downstairs pulls in a younger crowd and provides a popular venue for up-and-coming rock bands. Open seven days a week until 2am.

FITZSIMONS `25 G7`
East Essex Street, Temple Bar
Phone 677 9315
A large, split-level bar, designed along traditional lines with bare floorboards and plenty of exposed stonework, but the clientele is very cosmopolitan, as you would expect from a bar set in the heart of the Temple Bar area. A large screen comes into operation for major sporting events and, for the musically inclined, there is a traditional Irish band most nights of the week and even a bit of set dancing for frustrated Riverdance fans. The **Pier Nite Club** downstairs caters for those who prefer to dance with both feet on the floor.

FRONT LOUNGE/BACK LOUNGE `25 G7`
Parliament Street, Dublin 2
Whether it's Front Lounge or Back Lounge depends on which entrance you use, but style and sophistication are the watch words throughout. This is a good place to

escape the Temple Bar throng, sink into one of the comfy sofas or armchairs, and cast an appreciative eye over the art, sculpture, and your fellow poseurs. Not a gay pub, as such, but certainly popular with the gay community.

THE GAIETY THEATRE   `25 G8`
South King Street, Dublin 2
Phone 677 1717
Several Dublin theatres are turned over to late night clubbers on Friday and Saturday nights. The Gaiety makes use of the theatre bars to provide three floors of entertainment with different DJ's and live bands on each floor while cult films are screened in the main auditorium. Doors open at 11.15 pm. The music is mainly Latin & Salsa on Friday nights, Jazz & Soul on Saturdays. Bars stay open until 2.30am.

THE GLOBE   `25 G8`
11 South Great George's Street, Dublin 2
Phone 671 1220
One of the first in a long succession of Dublin café bars, but it still attracts a young, up-beat, fashion-conscious crowd. A relaxed atmosphere during the day, but things can become uncomfortably busy as the evening draws on. Jazz session on Sunday afternoons.

THE HARBOURMASTER BAR   `25 H7`
Phone 670 1688
Financial Services Centre, Dublin 1
If you like the contrast of old and new, you will like this place which is set in the old Dock Offices building, bang in the middle of the brand, spanking, new financial district, with acres of steel and glass peering down from above. The dimly lit interior, which has been sensitively converted to its present use, is populated by quite a few of the suits who work nearby, but the atmosphere is very laid back and unpretentious. Decent bar food is available or you can dine in a separate restaurant area which overlooks the dock basin outside.

THE HARCOURT HOTEL   `25 G8`
60-61 Harcourt Street, Dublin 2
Phone 878 3677
This fine Georgian building was once home to George Bernard Shaw, but live music every night of the week is the main attraction these days. Traditional, country, jazz and blues all feature on a regular basis, and there's also a post-gig nightclub, **Velvet**.

HOGAN'S   `25 G8`
35 George's Street, Dublin 2
Phone 677 5904
Stylish café bar which attracts a trendy crowd of young Dubliners, both straight and gay. Club downstairs.

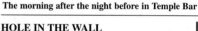
The morning after the night before in Temple Bar

HOLE IN THE WALL   `23 D7`
Phoenix Park, South Gate
Originally a coach house dating back to 1610, the Hole in the Wall is as close as you'll get to finding a pub within the 1700 acres of Dublin's Phoenix Park.

THE INTERNATIONAL   `25 G8`
23 Wicklow Street, Dublin 2
Phone 677 9250
A pub of two halves offering a nicely preserved Victorian bar downstairs and the popular Comedy Cellar upstairs (yes, *upstairs*) which acts as a venue for live bands as well as comedy. Wednesday is the main night for stand-up, Mondays for improv, and there are open mike spots for anybody wanting to make a total eedjit of themselves. Live music features every other night with rock, traditional, and rhythm & blues bands all appearing regularly.

IRISH FILM CENTRE   `25 G7`
6 Eustace Street, Temple Bar
Award winning architecture has transformed this Georgian building into a complex which includes two cinemas, a bookshop, and a bar cum restaurant which are all planned around a glass-covered courtyard. The food is innovative but reasonably priced and the clientele suitably arty with a tendency to wear anything, as long as it's black! Live music, mainly blues & jazz, and a late bar every Friday and Saturday night.

Mulligans - home to the best pint of Guinness in Dublin?

JOHNNY FOX'S
Glencullen, County Dublin
Phone 295 5647
Although Johnny Fox's is half an hour by car from the city centre, it is well worth the journey. Established back in 1798, the pub enjoys a picturesque setting in the Dublin Mountains and the accolade of being the highest licensed premises in Ireland. It also has a great reputation for its seafood and traditional music.

JURY'S HOTEL `32 J9`
Pembroke Road, Ballsbridge, Dublin 4
Phone 660 5000
The main hotel bar, Dubliner's, is worth a visit if you fancy some drawing room comfort. If it's Irish cabaret you are after, Jury's stages a nightly show of music, song and dance throughout the tourist season (except for Monday's) and, for insomniacs, the hotel's Coffee Dock stays open until 4.30am. Its proximity to Landsdowne Road means that the hotel is a hive of activity whenever a rugby international is being played.

KAVANAGH'S `17 G5`
Prospect Square, Glasnevin, Dublin 9
Known as the **"Gravediggers Arms"** due to its proximity to Prospect Cemetery, Dublin's main graveyard and the final resting place of many of Ireland's famous sons. The pub has been in the same family since 1833 during which time its traditional roots have been proudly preserved.

KIELY'S / CISS MADDEN'S `32 J10`
22-24 Donnybrook Road, Dublin 4
Kiely's is a pleasantly spacious bar, expensively refurbished along traditional lines with plenty of mahogany and stained glass. If you carry on through to the back, you will find Ciss Madden's, a more down to earth type of pub, which has its own separate entrance. The bar food is excellent.

THE KITCHEN (See the Clarence Hotel)

KITTY O'SHEA'S `26 J8`
23-25 Grand Canal Street Upper, Dublin 4
Phone 660 8050
Kitty O'Shea was the mistress of Charles Stewart Parnell, an association which cost him the leadership of the Home Rule Party back in 1890. The pub successfully evokes this era with its wooden snugs, stained glass, and a lively atmosphere. This is a classic Dublin pub which attracts customers from all walks of life but it it is especially popular with the rugby fraternity. There's live traditional music every night, a jazz brunch on Sundays and the bar food comes highly recommended.

LILLIE'S BORDELLO `25 G7`
Adam Court, Grafton Street, Dublin 2
Phone 679 9204
Probably the most exclusive nightclub in the city, you will have to be on good form to talk your way in on a Friday or Saturday night when it's supposedly "members only". Celebrity spotting is carried out in considerable comfort, with lots of sofas and red velvet armchairs contributing to the brothel theme. Open seven nights a week but things don't really get going until after the pubs shut.

THE LONG HALL `25 G8`
51 South Great George's Street, Dublin 2
Phone 475 1590
A long Victorian hall is more or less what you get, but it's the decor that makes this place a bit special. The bar itself is pure kitsch, ostentatious chandeliers hang from the ceiling, an array of antique time pieces add to the curious splendour, and all seem to combine against the odds to make this a delightful place. And to cap it all, the staff are friendly and eager to satisfy the thirst of their customers.

McDAID'S `25 G8`
3 Harry Street, Dublin 2
Phone 679 4395
Famous for being Brendan Behan's local back in the 1950's, but its location, just off Grafton Street, means that the literati are far outnumbered today by tourists and office workers.

McTURCAILLL'S `25 H7`
33 Tara Street, Dublin 2
The mock shop fronts which make up the facade at Askel McTurcaill's identify it as yet another Irish theme bar but, in this instance, the project has been undertaken with good taste and at considerable expense. The result is a very attractive bar which does

much to enhance an uninspiring location.

MEAN FIDDLER `25 G8`
26 Wexford Street, Dublin 2
Phone 475 8555
Younger sibling to its London namesake, this Mean Fiddler forsakes Dublin's obsession with the traditional look and goes for something a bit more stark and futuristic, along the lines of many of Manchester's post industrial-style café bars. Upstairs is a major late night venue for up and coming bands.

MOTHER REDCAP'S TAVERN `25 G8`
Back Lane, Christchurch, Dublin 8
Phone 453 3960
A shoe factory in a former life, Mother Redcap's is a large, two storied pub, refurbished in rustic fashion using timbers salvaged from an old flour mill. Lots of live music, mainly traditional, jazz and blues.

MULLIGAN'S `25 H7`
8 Poolbeg Street, Dublin 2
Phone 677 5582
Known as Mulligans of Poolbeg Street to distinguish it from the others, this pub dates back to1782 and has changed very little over the years, even retaining its gas lighting. With three slightly dilapidated bars and an upstairs lounge, this is essentially a pub with no frills, popular with students and journalists from the two national newspapers located nearby, and revered for the fact that it serves, arguably, the best pint of Guinness in Dublin. Former patrons include John F Kennedy who used to drop in while working for Hearst newspapers after World War II. There's no shortage of local characters among today's regulars, and the pub has even been immortalised on film, featuring as the local in "My Left Foot".

NEARY'S `25 G8`
1 Chatham Street, Dublin 2
Phone 677 8596
Situated close to the back door of the Gaiety Theatre, it is hardly surprising that Neary's is popular with both the acting fraternity and their audiences. The pub is easily recognised from outside by a distinctive pair of brass hands, each holding a glass lamp aloft on either side of the entrance. The ornate interior is Victorian with a busy bar downstairs and a quieter lounge upstairs.

THE NORSEMAN `25 G7`
27 Essex Street East, Temple Bar
Phone 671 5135
The Norseman was a popular pub long before Temple Bar became trendy. Much of its original character has

The Odeon - where work is an occupational hazard

survived the recent refurbishment, and it remains a comfortable place to enjoy a pint, although most of its customers seem to prefer the street outside during the summer months. There's a good session of Irish traditional music session on Tuesday night, and jazz sessions upstairs Sunday and Monday night.

THE ODEON `25 G8`
Harcourt Street, Dublin 2
What do you do with an old train station? In this case, convert it, very tastefully, into a bar which feels like it ought to be overlooking Barry's tea plantation. It's not quite Raffles Hotel, but everything is on a grand scale, with parquet floors and a cool interior. Ceiling fans seem conspicuous by their absence, but art-lined walls, comfy sofas and armchairs all add much to the laid back air. An outdoor terrace provides an ideal spot to sip a cold drink while contemplating just how good life can be as you watch the helter skelter of the real world outside. Food, mainly pizzas and pasta, is available at lunchtime and in the evening.

O'DONOGHUE'S `25 H8`
15 Merrion Row, Dublin 2
Phone 660 7194
One of Dublin's best known traditional bars, frequented by musicians, most notably members of the Dubliners. Getting to the bar can be a bit of a challenge

if you arrive at a busy time (which is virtually all of the time), but Irish enterprise overcomes such adversity with a strategically placed member of staff who stands on the counter so that you can shout your order as you come through the door! A courtyard area outside caters for the overspill. Traditional music sessions every night.

O'DWYER'S 25 H8
8 Lower Mount Street, Dublin 2
Phone 676 2887
Situated close to Merrion Square, O'Dwyer's is a spacious pub which is popular with the local business community at lunchtime and early evening. Pizza is a speciality of the house and, if you are in the mood to party until late, there's a nightclub in the basement.

THE OLD STAND 25 G8
37 Exchequer Street, Dublin 2
Phone 677 7220
Busy bar with a strong sporting tradition, especially where rugby and horseracing are concerned. Excellent bar food.

THE OLIVER ST JOHN GOGARTY 25 G7
58-59 Fleet Street, Temple Bar
Phone 671 1822
First established in 1850, and later named after the famous Irish surgeon, poet, and politician. Wearing his Senator's hat, it was Gogarty who offered the nation economic hope when he suggested that the crossing of a Friesan bull with a queen bee would result in a country flowing with milk and honey. Customers these days have to make do with a pint of the amber nectar, although a pint of the dark stuff is a more likely tipple. Gogarty's is a popular tourist haunt and you are sure to encounter the occasional 'stag group'. If you are a prospective groom in need of an aphrodisiac, £5 will buy you half a dozen oysters! There's also a daily diet of live traditional music, and a musical pub crawl starts upstairs at 7.30pm every evening (except for Friday) during the summer months. See page 89.

THE OLYMPIA 25 G7
74 Dame Street, Dublin 2
Phone 677 7744
A former music hall, the Olympia is Dublin's oldest theatre, but it becomes a concert venue with late bar from midnight on Friday and Saturday nights. Unreserved seating leaves you free to move around. The music tends to be rock or country.

O'NEILL'S 25 G7
Suffolk Street, Dublin 2
If you have just been in Bord Failte's impressive infor-

mation centre on Suffolk Street, then it's worth crossing the road to digest all the blurb and plan your itinerary over a pint in O'Neill's. This is a deceptively large, traditional style pub which attracts plenty of passing trade from nearby Grafton Street and Trinity College..

PADDY FLAHERTY'S 26 J8
51 Haddington Road, Ballsbridge, Dublin 4
Phone 660 8038
Self proclaimed "Irish Whiskey Pub", named after an early 20th century drink salesman who sold so much of the stuff that he lent his name to Paddy whiskey. Situated near to Lansdowne Road, this is a traditional Irish pub which is at its best when packed with the rugby fraternity on match days.

THE PALACE 25 G7
21 Fleet Street, Dublin 2
Phone 677 9290
Palace it may be, but a small one which has changed very little over many years. This is a great little pub with a very grand wooden bar, tiled floor and some nice leaded glass. Well worth following in the footsteps of the many literary figures who have passed through its doors and now adorn the walls of the back room.

THE POD 25 G8
Harcourt Street, Dublin 2
Phone 478 0225
When the PoD, or Place of Dance, opened in 1993, it quickly became one of Dublin's hippest clubs with style police on the door ready to refuse entry if you fail to make the sartorial grade! The club, which is located in two large stone vaults which used to form part of Harcourt Street Rail Station, still retains its popularity in the face of growing competition.

THE PORTERHOUSE 25 G7
16 Parliament Street, Dublin 2
Phone 679 8847
A pub and micro-brewery laid out on three busy floors. Their own brews are well worth a try, and the food is excellent too, especially when washed down with a pint of Oyster Stout or a glass or two of Brainblásta!

PRAVDA 25 G7
Liffey Street Lower, Dublin 1
It is good to see the north side of the river strike back against the bourgeoisie on the south bank! The truth, or the pravda, is that Moscow was never this trendy, with more varieties of vodka behind the bar than you could shake a stick at. It may look small from outside, but inside is cavernous, with the Russian theme not much in evidence until you reach the far end of the bar and glimpse the revolutionary murals. This is very much an

'in place' at the moment, and you may have to queue to get in at busy times, but the effort will be rewarded, especially if you can get one of the comfy seats upstairs where things are a bit more chilled out.

THE RED BOX
Harcourt Street, Dublin 2   `25 G8`
Phone 478 0210
Located directly above the PoD, its older sibling, the Red Box is currently one of the hottest venues in town, playing host to regular visits from British superclubs such as Cream.

RENARDS
South Frederick Street, Dublin 2   `25 H8`
Phone 677 5876
Clubbing seven nights a week with plenty of jazz and blues until the small hours. There's a dance floor in the basement, a café bar on the ground floor, and a VIP area on the first floor if you feel you warrant it.

RI-RA
Dame Court, Dublin 2   `25 G8`
Phone 679 7302
One of Dublin's major clubs, Rí-Rá (pronounced Ree-Raw) is a bit less exclusive than its main rivals, the **Kitchen** and the **PoD**, but this only serves to enhance the laid back atmosphere. The music includes house, hip-hop and ragga, and you are free to chill out upstairs in the **Globe Bar** after midnight.

RYAN'S
28 Parkgate Street, Dublin 8   `24 E7`
Phone 677 6097
Known as "Ryans of Parkgate Street" to distinguish it from the others, this is a fine example of an unspoilt Victorian pub, complete with snugs. Situated near to the entrance of Phoenix Park, regulars argue that Ryan's serves the finest pint in Dublin, a case which is strengthened by the fact that the Guinness Brewery lies just across the river.

THE SHELBOURNE HOTEL
St Stephen's Green   `25 H8`
Phone 676 6471
The Shelbourne may be the city's grandest hotel, but the two ground floor bars are thriving after-work meeting places for many of Dublin's movers and shakers, especially on Friday nights. The smaller **Horseshoe Bar** catches the overspill from the larger **Shelbourne Bar** which has its own entrance in Kildare Street. Both bars, like the rest of the hotel, retain an early 19th century elegance, although you have more chance of appreciating it during the daytime when things are a bit quieter.

SINNOTTS
South King Street, Dublin 2   `25 G8`
Phone 478 4698
Sinnotts is a large basement bar which has been likened to the bar in the TV sit-com, "Cheers". Although a relatively new pub, the decor is quite traditional with a tiled floor, high beamed ceiling, and panelled walls which are lined with numerous figures from Irish literature. Its location next to the St Stephen's Green Centre helps to make this is a busy bar during the day, and a daily diet of live Jazz & Blues until 2am ensures a good crowd after dark as well.

SLATTERY'S
129/130 Capel Street, Dublin 1   `25 G7`
Phone 872 7971
Situated north of the river between Henry Street and Abbey Street, Slattery's is a Victorian pub, lacking in glamour, but well loved as a venue for live music - Irish traditional downstairs, rock & blues in the upstairs lounge.

JJ SMYTH'S
12 Aungier Street, Dublin 2   `25 G8`
Phone 475 2565
Something of a Mecca for jazz and blues enthusiasts.

THE STAG'S HEAD
1 Dame Court, Dublin 2   `25 G8`
Phone 679 3701
A mosaic of a stag's head, embedded in the pavement opposite the Central Bank, alerts you to the fact that this jewel of a pub is hiding at the other end of the cobble-stoned passageway. Built in 1770, the Stag's Head has earned the rare distinction of featuring on an Irish postage stamp. The pub has changed very little since it was remodelled in 1895, with an impressive granite-topped bar, lots of carved mahogany, and eight stained glass windows promoting the stag theme. If you can't get a seat in the main bar, try the back room with its stained glass ceiling. The pub grub is plain, simple and delicious, and includes old favourites such as Irish stew and bacon & cabbage.

THE TEMPLE BAR
47/48 Temple Bar   `25 G7`
Phone 677 3807
Like the Norseman nearby, the Temple Bar is a 19th century stalwart which has seen a few changes in recent years. A modern extension successfully combines old with new, offering two pubs for the price of one, linked by 'The Temple Bar Garden' which is really just a courtyard area where you can catch the afternoon sun while enjoying some pretty decent pub grub. Things get increasingly raucous as the night wears on, and extend

Zanzibar - where the Liffey meets the Bosphorus

ed opening hours mean that you can grab a late pint and join the throng when many other bars have shut.

THE TEMPLE BAR MUSIC CENTRE 25 G7
Curved Street, Temple Bar
Phone 764 9202
The bar is only a small part of this broad-based, musical resource centre which includes recording studios, a Sound Training Centre, and a TV studio which doubles as a sizeable venue for live music and comedy.

THINGS MOTE 25 G7
Suffolk Street, Dublin 2
It is easy to pass along Suffolk Street and fail to recognise Things Mote as a pub, but do venture in because this is something of a hidden jewel. The interior resembles a large confessional with some fantastic wood carving and an amazing gold chandelier which would look at home in a Russian Orthodox church. Customers, mainly Dubliners rather than tourists, pack the pub after work and college.

THOMAS CROWE 32 K9
Merrion Road, Ballsbridge, Dublin 4
A convenient watering hole if you are heading to a match at nearby Lansdowne Road. This is an attractive

pub which is proud of its sporting connections judging by the rugby memorabilia which adorn the walls.

THOMAS READ 25 G7
4 Parliament Street, Dublin 2
Phone 670 7220
From the awnings outside to the ceiling fans, wooden floors, bentwood chairs and the whiff of Gauloise inside, you could be forgiven for imagining that you are in Paris rather than across the road from Dublin Castle. Lively café bar, good food and great coffee make Thomas Read's a fashionable spot to while away the day or night.

TONER'S 25 H8
139 Lower Baggot Street, Dublin 2
Phone 676 3090
Not far from St Stephen's Green, Toner's is one of Dublin's most characterful pubs, an authentic spirit grocers which concentrates more on the spirits than the groceries these days. Stone floors add to the rustic feel, and some interesting artefacts help to make it the time capsule that it is.

TURK'S HEAD 25 G7
Parliament Street, Dublin 2
Phone 679 2567
The interior is a slightly over-the-top tribute to Gaudi, but it's all good fun and the party continues until late in the nightclub downstairs.

WHELAN'S 25 G8
25 Wexford Street, Dublin 2
Phone 478 0766
An early Victorian pub which was restored to former glories with the help of some major renovation back in 1989. Best known, however, as one of the best musical venues in Dublin, staging live performances every night of the week. Rock, blues, and traditional tastes are all catered for, and there's always an enthusiastic crowd of locals and visitors to lap up the entertainment.

ZANZIBAR 25 G7
Ormond Quay Lower, Dublin 1
Zanzibar, along with Pravda just along the road, is doing much to draw the Temple Bar crowd across the river although, when you first see inside, you may feel that you have just crossed the Bosphorus rather than the Liffey. The interior seems to have been designed on a 'bizarre bazaar' theme, with palm trees lining a bar so long that it seems to disappear into the distance. It's all very lavish, and on a grand scale, but the overall effect works extremely well. This is one of the few Dublin pubs which you might have to queue to get into, but a visit is highly recommended.

There are many hundreds of restaurants and cafés to choose from in Dublin, and this guide attempts to select about 100 of the best. This process is bound to be subjective but no apologies are made for that. After all, how many times have you eaten at a restaurant because it happened to be recommended to you by somebody else?

All establishments featured have been tried out, often frequently, by somebody connected with the Dublin Street Atlas & Guide. They have been selected by people who enjoy good food and drink, bearing in mind price, location and diversity. These places are the ones that we have enjoyed most - the ones that we recommend to friends and relatives. They don't always agree, and perhaps you won't either, but that's what being subjective is all about! Having said that, we would be keen to hear your own recommendations or any objections that you might have regarding any of our choices.

What can be said, without fear of contradiction, is that the restaurant scene in Dublin has been transformed over the past ten years. Choice and quality have improved tremendously, and this trend looks set to continue. In terms of culinary diversity, price and atmosphere, Dublin restaurants can hold their own against most other European capitals.

Many are mentioned in the growing array of good food guides. These publications all have their good points but, invariably, one area of contention is their attempts to estimate the likely cost of a meal. We have all had the experience of going somewhere supposedly "cheap & cheerful" only to find that a couple of drinks and a shared bottle of wine can have a strange effect on the bill. On the other hand, there are occasions when you may have taken advantage of a very reasonable fixed price menu, and left with both your conscience and the contents of your wallet largely intact!

When you add in lunchtime and early evening specials, fixed-price menus, and happy hours, attempts to estimate price often tend to be in vain. The system adopted for this guide, therefore, is rather broad-brush in its approach, attempting to categorise a restaurant as expensive, moderate or cheap.

"Expensive" restaurants are those where you can expect the final bill to exceed £25 per head. If you eat somewhere categorised as "cheap", you will, more often than not, escape for under a tenner. The final bill at a restaurant falling into the moderate category should fall somewhere between £10 and £25, bearing in mind all the caveats mentioned earlier.

Finally, the golden rule when using this guide is to phone first! All the information included was gathered at the end of 1998, but restaurants come and go,

PRICE RATING

£   Cheap (usually under £10 per head)

££   Moderate (between £10 and £25)

£££   Expensive (£25+)

change ownership, chefs, menus, opening hours and much else, so it's best to check with the restaurant before turning up.

101 TALBOT `25 H7`
100-102 Talbot Street, Dublin1
Phone 874 5011
Price Rating: ££
Conveniently located for the Abbey and Gate Theatres, Talbot Street seems an unlikely place to go looking for good food but upstairs at number 101 soon changes that view. The eating space is bright, spacious, and informal, with newspapers on hand in case you are just popping in for coffee and a snack. The lunch and dinner menus don't stay the same for long but the food is always wholesome and delicious with plenty of choice for vegetarians. *Opening Times: Tues-Sat 10am-11pm*

ADRIAN'S `13 V2`
8 Abbey Street, Howth
Phone 839 1696
Price Rating: ££
Look for the large Victorian terrace, painted on the outside to resemble an aquarium as if to compensate for the fact that it narrowly misses out on a sea view. There's more to life than a sea view, however, as you will discover when you taste the food which inventively combines some fine local ingredients from both land and sea. *Opening Times: Mon-Sat 12.30pm-3pm & 6pm-9.30pm; Sun 6pm-8pm*

AL BOSCHETTO `32 J9`
Beatty's Avenue, Ballsbridge
Price Rating: ££
A little bit of Tuscany in the heart of Ballsbridge (OK, so you may have to use a little bit of imagination) where you can expect good, honest, Italian food at rea-

sonable prices.

AR VICOLETTO `25 G7`
5 Crow Street, Temple Bar
Phone 670 8662
Price Rating: ££
Simple Italian cooking which allows the flavour of the best, sun-rich ingredients to do the talking. The atmosphere is relaxed and unpretentious, and the prices are relatively inexpensive. *Opening Times: Mon-Sat 12noon-12midnight; Sun 2pm-12midnight*

AVENUE `32 J10`
1 Belmont Avenue, Donnybrook, Dublin 4
Phone 260 3738
Price Rating: ££
Dublin has opened some very good restaurants in recent years but, when it comes to designer cool, Avenue surpasses most. The main building, which is reached across an open courtyard with outdoor seating, is divided between a café bar area and a rather sumptuous bistro which seats 160 on two levels. The decor is similar throughout, with an emphasis on lots of natural light and bold colours, both on the walls and upholstery. The café and bistro have separate menus, the latter reflecting the credentials of the head chef who used to work at a Michelin Star establishment. Pedigree is reflected in the bill, but at least you get to calculate the damage in Euros as well as pounds. *Café is open Mon-Sun 10am-6pm; Restaurant is open Mon-Sat 6pm-11pm; Sun 12noon-4pm*

AYUMI-YA `39 N13`
Newpark Centre, Newtownpark Avenue, Blackrock
Phone 283 1767
Price Rating: ££
Opening Times: Mon-Sat 6pm-11pm; Sun 5.30pm-9.45pm. The Ayumi-Ya was Ireland's first Japanese restaurant when it opened in 1983 and it remains the standard bearer with cooking, service, and surroundings which are truly authentic. With a menu which ranges from sushi and tempura to char-grilled chicken and beef teriyaki dishes, there is a selection to suit all tastes. You can opt to dine Japanese-style, sitting on the floor at low tables, or you can stay with the table and chair combo if you prefer a loftier vantage point. The **Ayumi-Ya Steakhouse**, a sister restaurant situated closer to the city centre on Lower Baggot Street, offers a less traditional, but no less satisfying, alternative (phone 662 0233).

BT2 `25 G8`
Grafton Street, Dublin 2
Price Rating: £
If shopping for D&G, Armani, and Prada gives you a thirst (or you simply want to escape doing so in the first place) the café at BT2 is a suitably hip watering hole to stop and contemplate the need for a new image.

BAD ASS CAFE `25 G7`
9-11 Crown Alley, Temple Bar
Phone 671 2596
Price Rating : £
The Bad Ass, despite its bad jokes, remains a Temple Bar institution which attracts a mainly young crowd to its warehouse-style cafeteria. From the bronze hoofprints in the pavement outside to the pulley system inside which transports your order to the kitchen, things are that little bit different here. The menu suits a tight budget while offering some pretty decent pizzas, pasta, burgers and salads. Sinead O'Connor used to wait tables here - so, make a note of the face that serves you, just for future reference. *Opening Times: Mon-Sun 9am-11pm*

BELLA CUBA `32 J9`
Ballsbridge Terrace, Dublin 4
Phone 660 5539
Price Rating: ££
Small, upstairs, restaurant where, with the help of a couple of daiquiris and the Cuban jazz soundtrack, you can taste a little bit of Havana without breaking any embargoes.

BESHOFF'S `25 G7`
14 Westmoreland Street, Dublin 2
Price Rating : £
A good, old fashioned, fish and chip shop where choice varies according to the catch of the day, and the food comes on a plate instead of being wrapped in yesterday's newspaper. A good plaice(?) to feed hungry snappers without breaking the bank. Second outlet, more modern in style, at the International Food Court on Upper O'Connell Street. *Opening Times: Mon-Sun 11am-3am*

BEWLEY'S ORIENTAL CAFE `25 G8`
78/79 Grafton Street, Dublin 2
Phone 677 6761
Price Rating : £
Once Mungo Bewley and his Quaker family set foot on Irish shores back in the 1840's, they spotted a gap in the caffeine market, and Bewley's has been a Dublin institution ever since. The flagship outlet on Grafton Street, famed for Harry Clarke's stained glass and the smell of roasting coffee, has recently benefited from a £4m refit. Continental café style table service is now the order of the day on the ground floor, while first floor customers dine under a new skylit ceiling in the Atrium Café which operates on a buffet basis. The James Joyce Room has survived the overhaul, with the added advantage of an alcohol licence which means that you can choose from a wide-ranging, well-priced, wine list, with most of the

24 wines offered by the glass as well as by the bottle. The new regime aims to broaden the appeal and attract the evening diner, but Bewley's remains at its best as a refuge from the hurly-burly where you can sip your favourite blend of freshly brewed tea or coffee and nibble on something from the mouthwatering selection of home-baked pastries. A table by the window on the first floor Mezzanine still offers an ideal location to watch the world go by while enjoying some good Irish fare such as smoked salmon on wheaten bread. Among several other branches, **Westmoreland Street** and **Mary Street** have also been revamped, but closing time tends to come earlier than on Grafton Street. *Opening Times: Sun-Thurs 8am-1am; Fri-Sat 7.30am-5am*

BILLBOARD CAFE `25 G8`
43 Lower Camden Street, Dublin 2
Phone 475 5047
Price Rating: £
Laid back café, popular with clubbers for the fact that it stays open 24 hours a day at weekends. And if your stomach thinks your throat's been cut, you can reassure it with an Irish breakfast which is served all day.

BLAZING SALADS II `25 G8`
Powerscourt Townhouse, Clarendon St, Dublin 2
Phone 671 9552
Price Rating: £
Located on the first floor of a fine Georgian townhouse which has been tastefully converted into a shopping mall, the dining area overlooks an atrium below where live piano music soothes the savage breast of the lunchtime shopper. Eco warriors will be happy with touches such as a napkin dispenser which implores you to "Think of the trees!", but this is a place with much wider appeal, where you can choose from a wholesome range of hot and cold vegetarian dishes, and eat your fill for around a fiver. *Opening Times: Mon-Sat 9.30am-6pm*

BRUNO'S `25 G7`
30 East Essex Street, Temple Bar
Phone 670 6767
Price Rating: ££
Situated in the heart of Temple Bar, Bruno's modern French cuisine and cool decor tends to attract some serious foodies. Space is limited, but well planned, and the atmosphere is generally pretty lively. There's not a great deal of choice for vegetarians, but omnivores will not be disappointed. *Opening Times: 12noon-12midnight*

CAFE AURIGA `25 G7`
Temple Bar Square, Dublin 2
Phone 671 8228
Price Rating: ££
Makes the most of its prime location, looking out

Surfers and grazers at Cyberia Cafe

through large plate glass windows onto Dublin's busiest square below. The food, like the setting, is modern and trendy, and romantic cheapskates can take comfort in an early evening menu priced at £9.95 per head. *Opening Times: Mon-Sat 12noon-11pm*

CAFE IRIE `25 G7`
11 Upper Fownes Street, Temple Bar
Price Rating: £
Small, slightly anarchic in appearance, but a very enjoyable spot to eat an organic breakfast or lunch for under a fiver.

CAFE JAVA `25 G8`
5 South Anne Street, Dublin 2
Phone 670 7239
Price Rating: £
Stylish café laid out on two floors with lots of stripped wood, white walls, and a glass facade which proudly reveals its Polynesian murals to the outside world. Good for breakfast, lunch and afternoon tea, and a prime spot for sipping cappuccino while watching the world go by. Another branch on 145 Leeson Street. *Opening Times: Mon-Fri 7.45am-7pm (8pm Thurs); Sat 9am-6pm; Sun 10am-6pm*

CAFE ROUGE `25 G8`
1 St Andrew's Street, Dublin 2
Phone 679 1357
Price Rating: ££
Francophiles should note that Café Rouge is part of a

The Bad Ass Cafe - a Temple Bar institution

successful British chain which knows a thing or two about attracting customers. The familiar formula of a well designed interior, an interesting menu and attentive service works the trick yet again. *Opening Times: Mon-Sat 10am-11pm; Sun 10am-10.30pm*

CAPTAIN AMERICA'S `25 G8`
44 Grafton Street, Dublin 2
Phone 671 5266
Price Rating: £
Many Dubliners associate this place with a guy whose job it was to dress as Captain America, stand rigid for hours on Grafton Street, and amuse/terrorise passers-by occasionally springing to life. Planet Hollywood may have arrived, but Captain America fights on with his armoury of burgers and rock memorabilia which continues to pull in a mainly youthful clientele. *Opening Times: Mon-Sun 12noon-1am*

CASA PASTA `13 V2`
12 Harbour Road, Howth
Phone 839 3823
Price Rating: £
A very pleasant setting overlooking Howth yacht club and beyond, a great selection of pasta including lots of seafood options, and all at pretty reasonable prices. The formula has been successfully repeated with the opening of a second branch down the road in Contarf. *Opening Times: Mon-Sat 6pm-12midnight; Sun 1pm-11pm*

CEDAR TREE `25 G8`
11 St Andrew's Street, Dublin 2
Phone 677 2121
Price Rating : ££
Highly rated Lebanese food. Choose from one of the mezzes (set menu for minimum of two people, including a vegetarian option) if you want to sample a wide range of dishes at a reasonable price. Belly dancing at weekends. *Opening Times: Mon-Sat 12noon-12midnight; Sun 12noon-11pm*

CHAMELEON `25 G7`
1 Fownes Street Lower, Temple Bar
Phone 671 0362
Price Rating: ££
Intimate Indonesian restaurant where the fact that the owners cook and serve the food helps to guarantee an enjoyable experience. The house speciality is *rijst-tafel*, or rice-table, which is a banquet of assorted dishes which reflect the many distinct cuisines from some of the thousands of Indonesian islands. Meat, fish, rice and noodles are the staple ingredients, and there are separate combinations for vegetarians and fish lovers. *Opening Times: Tues-Sun 5pm-11pm*

CHANDNI `32 J9`
174 Pembroke Road, Ballsbridge, Dublin 4
Phone 668 1458
Price Rating: ££
Excellent Indian food, including plenty of seafood and vegetarian options, served up in pleasant surroundings. Not cheap but well worth the price. *Opening Times: Mon-Fri 12.30pm-2.30pm; Mon-Sun 6pm-12midnight*

CHAPTER ONE `17 G8`
18/19 Parnell Square, Dublin 1
Phone 873 2266
Price Rating: £££
Situated in a vaulted cellar underneath Dublin Writers Museum, the restaurant continues the literary theme which prevails upstairs and combines it with some fine international cuisine. With its proximity to the Gate and the Abbey, this is a popular choice for theatre-goers, some of whom come early for a starter and main course and return after the show for dessert. The wine list is extensive but focuses mainly on familiar classics. *Opening Times: Mon-Fri 12.30pm-2.30pm; Tues-Sat 6pm-11pm*

CHEZ JULES `25 H7`
D'Olier Chambers, 16a D'Olier Street, Dublin 2
Phone 677 0499
Price Rating : ££
French-style bistro which caters well for large groups with its long communal tables and informal atmosphere. The menu doesn't stay the same for long but the choice

is usually original and the food is always delicious. *Opening Times: Mon-Fri 12noon-3pm & 5pm-11pm; Sat 1pm-11pm; Sun 1pm-10pm*

CHILI CLUB `25 G8`
1 Anne's Lane, Dublin 2
Phone 677 3721
Price Rating: ££
Tucked away, just off South Anne Street, the Thai chefs at the Chili Club ensure that the food is authentically hot and spicy, yet easy on the palate. Pre-theatre menu at £13.50 per head between 6pm and 7pm. *Opening Times: Mon-Sat 12.30-2.30; Mon-Sun 6pm til late*

CHINA-SICHUAN RESTAURANT `38 L14`
4 Kilmacud Road Lower
Phone 288 4817
Price Rating : ££
Located in the suburb of Stillorgan, this is Chinese food worth going that little bit out of your way for. The chefs, like many of the ingredients, are from Sichuan province in western China and the cooking delivers an authentic taste characterised by strong flavours (chillies are an essential ingredient in many Sichuan dishes). *Opening Times: Mon-Fri/Sun 12.30-2.30; Mon-Sun 6pm-11pm.*

CITRUS `13 V2`
Harbour Road, Howth
Phone 832 0200
Price Rating: ££
A modified, Thai restaurant which enjoys a very pleasant seaside setting just opposite Howth yacht club. The emphasis is on a modern approach to both the interior and the cooking. The menu takes advantage of the ready supply of fresh seafood which is landed every day on Howth pier, and some outdoor seating allows you to make the most of the location, weather permitting. *Open for lunch 11.30-3pm; dinner from 6pm*

THE COMMONS `25 H8`
85/86 St Stephen's Green, Dublin 2
Phone 475 2597
Price Rating: £££+
The Commons enjoys an enviable location in the basement of Newman House, one of Dublin's finest Georgian buildings. Weather permitting, you can sip an aperitif in the courtyard which is surrounded by five acres of private garden. The decor inside is stylish with rugs covering stone floors and walls lined with contemporary Irish art inspired by James Joyce who studied at the former university upstairs. The French cuisine matches the most exacting of standards while the

chez jules
RESTAURANT FRANCAIS

D'Olier Chambers, 16a D'Olier Street, Dublin 2
Telephone 677 0499

atmosphere reflects the serenity of the setting. *Opening Times: Mon-Fri 12.30pm-2.15pm; Mon-Sat 7pm-10pm*

COOKE'S CAFE & THE RHINO ROOM `25 G8`
14 South William Street, Dublin 2
Phone 679 0536
Price Rating : £££
This fashionable restaurant forms the nucleus of a mini culinary empire which includes a food hall across the street and bakeries in Francis Street and Dawson Street. Not one to rest on its laurels, the Rhino Room upstairs is the latest innovation, offering a New York-style grill bar which has quickly become one of the in-places to be seen. Downstairs remains as chic as ever, with a strong Mediterranean influence evident in both the cooking and the decor. Seafood features prominently on the menu and the home-baked breads and desserts come highly recommended. *Opening Times: Mon-Sun 12.30pm 'til late*

CORNUCOPIA `25 G8`
19 Wicklow Street, Dublin 2
Phone 677 7583
Price Rating: £
Popular vegetarian restaurant serving a wide selection

of imaginative dishes at very reasonable prices. *Opening Times: Mon-Sat 9am-8pm (until 9pm Thurs and until 10pm Fri & Sat)*

CYBERIA CAFE `25 G7`
Temple Lane, Temple Bar
Price Rating: £
Small, internet café, usually packed to the gills with grazers and surfers.

DISH `25 G7`
2 Crow Street, Temple Bar
Phone 671 1248
Price Rating: ££
Dish has quickly established itself as one of the most fashionable restaurants in Dublin. The dining room is light and airy, set a few feet above street level, with plenty of individual touches, not least a couple aluminium ventilation ducts on the ceiling which you half expect somebody to peer out of as you are eating your meal. The food is beautifully cooked and presented and the service is friendly and efficient. Set lunch £8.95. *Opening Times: Mon-Sun 12noon-11.30pm*

DOBBINS WINE BISTRO `25 H8`
15 Stephen's Lane, Dublin 2
Phone 676 4679
Popular choice when it comes to the long business lunch, or dinner for that matter. Good food, fine wine, and a very well run operation. *Opening Times: Mon-Fri 12.30pm-3pm; Tues-Sat 7.30pm-11.30pm*

DON ANGEL `25 H7`
7 D'Olier St, Dublin 2
Phone 679 3859
Spanish owned and run, Don Angel must be doing things the authentic way judging by the numbers of Spanish nationals who manage to find their way here. The menu concentrates on tapas, but there are the usual stalwarts such as paella if you fancy something more substantial. *Opening Times: Mon-Thurs 12noon-10pm; Fri-Sat 12noon-11pm; Sun 5pm-10pm*

EASTERN TANDOORI `25 G8`
34-35 South William Street, Dublin 2
Phone 671 0428
Price Rating: ££
Excellent Indian cuisine served up in very comfortable, but quite formal, surroundings. Everything about this place is rather discreet, except perhaps for the staff uniforms. *Opening Times: Mon-Sat 12noon-2.30pm & 6pm-12midnight; Sun 6pm-11.30pm*

EDEN `25 G7`
Meeting House Square, Temple Bar
Phone 670 5372

Price Rating: ££
This is no shrinking violet. The post-modern design exudes self-confidence, and first sight of the outdoor terrace overlooking the square immediately alerts you to the fact that this is somewhere cool and hip, somewhere to see and to be seen. The cooking is in sync with the surroundings, modern and imaginative. *Opening Times: Tues-Sun 12noon-late*

ELEPHANT & CASTLE `25 G7`
18 Temple Bar, Dublin 2
Phone 679 3121
Price Rating : ££
American style cooking served up in bright, informal surroundings by friendly staff - the combination is familiar, but nowhere else in Dublin has achieved such a successful blend, judging by the busy atmosphere which lasts the whole day long. The house speciality is the "elephantburger" but alternatives include an exhaustive selection of omelettes, and some excellent salads and pasta dishes. The spicy chicken wings make a delicious starter but the portion seems to be designed to satisfy the appetite of a Texan oilman, so it might be a good idea to share. Reservations are not accepted, but you can put your name on the waiting list if there isn't a table and pop over the road for a drink while you're waiting. *Opening Times: Mon-Fri 8am-11.30pm; Sat 10.30am-11.30pm; Sun 12noon-11.30pm*

ENVY CAPPUCCINO BAR `25 G7`
13 Crown Alley, Temple Bar
Phone 670 3161
Escape the hustle & bustle outside and seek sanctuary in this very cool, relaxing space, bathed in soft light. Works best as an excellent cappuccino stop but, if you decide to dwell a bit longer, there's food and wine on offer to sustain you throughout the day and long into the night. *Opening Times: Sun-Wed until 7pm; Thurs until 11pm; Fri-Sat until 4am*

ERNIE'S `32 J10`
Mulberry Gardens, Donnybrook, Dublin 4
Phone 269 3260
Price Rating: £££
Elegant restaurant overlooking pretty, floodlit gardens, and decorated with a fine collection of Irish art. Classical French cuisine and very attentive service. *Opening Times: Tues-Fri 12.30pm-2pm & 7.30pm-10.15pm; Sat 7.30pm-10.15pm*

FANS `25 G7`
60 Dame Street, Dublin 2
Phone 679 4263
Price Rating: ££
Cantonese cooking and a menu which offers an imaginative choice including some excellent dim sum.

Opening Times: Mon-Sun 12.30pm-2.15pm & 6.30pm-12midnight

FITZERS `25 G8`
51 Dawson Street, Dublin 2
Phone 677 1155
Price Rating: ££
Fitzers have several branches around the city and all are highly recommended for their tasteful interiors and their ability to deliver interesting food at sensible prices. Dawson Street offers separate menus for brunch, lunch and dinner in ascending order of price. The bright and sunny decor is in keeping with the Cal-Ital style of cooking, and there are few better places in town to enjoy a relaxed brunch and the Sunday papers. Other branches: Temple Bar Square; RDS, Ballsbridge; National Gallery, Merrion Square West. *Dawson Street Opening Times: Mon-Sat 12noon-4pm & 5.30pm-11.30pm; Sun 11am-11pm*

FUSION `32 K9`
Merrion Road, Ballsbridge, Dublin 4
Phone 667 1963
Price Rating: ££
Ultra-trendy, metropolitan café cum wine bar serving a familiar but tasty range of modern, international cuisine. *Opening Times: Mon 10.30-6.30; Tues-Fri 10.30am-10.30pm; Sat 11am-5pm & 6.30pm-10.30pm; Sun 11am-5pm*

GALLAGHER'S BOXTY HOUSE `25 G7`
20-21 Temple Bar
Phone 677 2762
Price Rating : ££
Traditional Irish cooking in a homely setting which attracts tourists like bees to honey. For those unfamiliar with the concept, the boxty is a kind of potato pancake which comes stuffed with a variety of fillings which include beef, lamb, chicken and fish. Other local specialities include Irish stew, bacon and cabbage, and champ (mashed potato with spring onion). It may not be *haute cuisine* but it is satisfying, and the lively atmosphere, traditional music, and friendly service help to keep Gallaghers one of the busiest places in town. *Opening Times: Mon-Sun 12noon-11.30pm*

GOTHAM CAFE `25 G8`
8 South Anne Street, Dublin 2
Phone 679 5266
Price Rating: £
New York theme cafe which is always buzzing, partly due to it's location just off Grafton Street, but mainly because its customers keep coming back to sample the gourmet pizzas, interesting pastas and salads, and the warm and friendly atmosphere. *Opening Times: Mon-Sat 12noon-12midnight*

The Elephant & Castle in Temple Bar

IL BACCARO `25 G7`
Diceman's Corner, Meeting House Square
Temple Bar
Phone 671 4597
Price Rating: £
Meeting House Square may be Dublin's newest piazza but, when you walk down the few steps into Il Baccaro, you may feel that you have entered some ancient drinking vault in the bowels of Prague rather than Dublin. Don't be deceived by the dimly lit interior, however, because this is a place to have fun, with friendly Italian staff on hand to keep the warm house red flowing by the carafe. The food is plain, simple, but highly recommended and, if you prefer life above ground, there are a few tables outside in the summer.

IMAGE GALLERY `25 G7`
25 East Essex Street, Temple Bar
Phone 679 3393
Price Rating : £
A good spot to pop into for coffee and a sandwich, not to mention a quick read of their newspapers and a look at the interesting photographic prints on show. *Opening Times: Mon-Wed 9.30am-7pm; Thurs-Sat 9.30am-11pm*

IMPERIAL CHINESE RESTAURANT `25 G8`
13 Wicklow Street, Dublin 2
Phone 677 2719
Price Rating: ££
Enjoyable Cantonese cuisine at any time, but Sunday tends to be the day when members of the Chinese community arrive in force to partake of the legendary dim sum. *Opening Times: Mon-Sun 12noon-12midnight*

INDEPENDENT PIZZA COMPANY `17 H5`
46 Lower Drumcondra Road, Dublin 9
Phone 830 2044
Price Rating: £
Situated on the airport road, this is a busy, friendly, local

Kapriol has been Dublin's finest Italian restaurant for over 20 years. Classic Northern Italian menu, specialising in seafood & serving DUBLIN'S LARGEST PRAWNS Pre theatre set menu from £16.95. Mention this ad when you book & we will give you a complimentary aperitif on arrival.

45 Lower Camden St, Dublin 2. Tel 475 1235

pizzeria which has been serving some of the tastiest pizzas in town since 1984. *Opening Times: Sun-Thurs 12noon-12.30am; Fri & Sat 12noon-1am*

IRISH FILM CENTRE   `25 G7`
6 Eustace Street, Temple Bar
Phone 677 8788
Price Rating : ££
The Irish Film Centre is described in more detail on page 93 but it warrants a special mention for its food which is served every day. The lunch and dinner menus are constantly changing but always innovative, and you can enjoy a great lunch for a fiver.

JOHNNY FOX'S FAMOUS SEAFOOD KITCHEN
Glencullen, Co Dublin. Phone 295 5647
Price Rating : ££
Like the Irish Film Centre above, Johnny Fox's is covered elsewhere on page 94 , but it also warrants a special mention for its delicious seafood and picturesque setting. *Opening Times: Mon-Sat 12noon-10pm; Sun 4pm-10pm*

JUDGE ROY BEAN'S   `25 H8`
45-47 Nassau Street, Dublin 2. Phone 679 7539
Price Range : ££
Located at the lower end of Grafton Street, this long established bar cum Tex/Mex restaurant offers convenient sanctuary from the hordes of shoppers that dominate this area of town. *Opening Times: Mon-Sun12noon-12midnight*

JUICE   `25 G8`
South Great George's Street, Dublin 2
Phone 475 7856
Price Rating : ££
The cutting edge of vegetarianism, at least where the trendy interior is concerned. The food includes a selection of tapas and a wide range of more familiar dishes, from veggie lasagne to Thai curry. Abandon any notion that vegetarian food is not filling - the portions are huge - so, if you are opting for a starter, it might be a good idea to share one. Wine is available, but don't leave without trying something from the fresh juice bar. *Opening Times: Mon-Fri 12noon-10pm; Sat 12.30pm-4am; Sun 12.30pm-10pm*

KAFFEE KLATSCH   `25 G8`
Westbury Mall, Harry Street, Dublin 2
Coffee is big business in Dublin these days, and Kaffee Klatsch has added to a growing array of very smart, ultra-modern pit stops where you can interrupt your retail therapy, rest your weary limbs, and indulge yourself in an excellent cup of coffee, a mouth-watering snack, and a healthy session of people watching.

KAFFE MOKA   `25 G8`
39 South William Street
Phone 679 8475
Price Rating : £
Recently extended to keep pace with demand, Kaffe Moka is many people's favourite coffee house in Dublin. Facilities include a library and games room, and the atmosphere is always warm and friendly which helps to keep things busy no matter what the time of day or night. Open daily until 4am.

KAPRIOL   `25 G8`
45 Camden Street Lower, Dublin 2
Phone 475 1235
Price Rating : ££
The Kapriol is a very traditional restaurant which has been around for many years. The classic Italian cooking is as good as you will find in Dublin and things are run very much as a family affair which helps to ensure a warm welcome and a loyal following. *Opening Times: Tues-Sat 6.30pm-12midnight.*

KILKENNY KITCHEN   `25 H8`
6 Nassau Street, Dublin 2
Phone 677 7066
Price Range : £
Situated on the first floor of the Kilkenny Shop, famous

for its range of Irish clothing and craft goods, the Kilkenny Kitchen provides a good range of wholesome lunches backed up by an interesting variety of home baked breads, cakes and biscuits which you can buy to eat or take home. Both shop and restaurant have recently undergone major refurbishment and the new look is very contemporary and pleasing on the eye. A small 'food hall' has been added upstairs which stocks a selection of hand made chocolates and other such treats. Self service remains the order of the day for the endless stream of hungry shoppers and office workers, but a table by the window allows you to gaze into the more peaceful world of Trinity College. *Opening Times: Mon-Sat 9am-6pm (until 8pm on Thurs)*

Enjoy a spectacular sea view upstairs at the King Sitric

KING SITRIC `13 V2`
East Pier, Howth
Phone 832 5235
Price Rating: £££
When you arrive in Howth for the first time you will find it difficult to believe that you are only 20 minutes from the centre of Dublin. Set in an old harbour master's house, the King Sitric takes full advantage of its location with spectacular views over Balscadden Bay. The upstairs seafood bar, which consists of half a dozen tables crammed into a modern extension, offers the best views, while the restaurant downstairs is more formal in atmosphere. The menu is dominated by whatever the Howth fishing fleet manages to catch earlier that day - the restaurant even has its own lobster and crab pots - but there are a few alternatives. Lunch costs from around £10 but dinner is more of a treat, with the fixed price menu coming in at £28 per head before you have chosen from the many fine wines on offer. With its long established and well earned reputation, however, you are unlikely to regret your decision to dine here. *Opening Times: Mon-Sat 12noon-3pm (May to September) & 6.30-11pm (all year)*

KITES CHINESE RESTAURANT `32 J9`
Ballsbridge Terrace, Dublin 4
Phone 660 7415
Price Rating: ££
Located in a Georgian terrace in fashionable Ballsbridge, Kites is an up-market Chinese restaurant offering a wide range of Cantonese cuisine including several fish dishes. The dim sum at £20 per head (minimum of two people) isn't cheap but it's a good option for the inquisitive palate.

LA PALOMA `25 G7`
17b Asdills Row, Temple Bar
Phone 677 7392
Price Rating : ££
Spanish restaurant and tapas bar decorated with murals which are likely to make Miro turn in his grave - fortu-

nately, the food and the atmosphere more than make amends. Spanish dancing Thursday & Friday nights. *Opening Times: Mon-Sun 12noon-1am*

LA STAMPA `25 H8`
35 Dawson Street, Dublin 2
Phone 677 8611
Price Rating : £££
La Stampa is widely regarded as one of the finest restaurants in Ireland. The dining room started life as the ballroom of a 19th century guildhall and the decor retains much of the original grandeur. Don't be misled by the Italian name, the cuisine at La Stampa is essentially French and the food lives up to very high expectations. The clientele includes many of Dublin's movers and shakers but the atmosphere is generally lively and informal - an ideal place to see and to be seen. The bistro downstairs serves a slightly different menu in more intimate surroundings. *Opening Times: Mon-Fri 12.30pm-2.30pm; Mon-Sun 6.30pm-11.30pm.*

LANGKAWI `31 H9`
46 Upper Baggot Street, Dublin 2
Phone 668 2760
Price Rating: ££
Like Malaysia itself, the cuisine at Langkawi reflects a combination of Malay, Chinese and Indian influences. Although much of the food can be hot and spicy, milder alternatives such as satay are also on offer. *Opening Times: Mon-Fri 12.30pm-2pm & 6pm-11.30pm; Sat 6pm-11.30pm*

LE COQ HARDI `32 J9`
35 Pembroke Road, Dublin 4
Phone 668 4130
Price Rating: £££+
The Georgian splendour should be enough to tell you that this is the territory of serious food and wine buffs, and you will not be disappointed on either score as long

as you can afford to ignore the cost. The French cuisine is rated among the very best in Dublin and the menu is complimented by an award winning wine cellar. *Opening Times: Mon-Fri 12.30pm-3pm; Mon-Sat 7pm-11pm*

LE VIGNERON `25 G7`
6 Cope Street, Temple Bar
Phone 671 5740
Price Rating: ££
Bistro downstairs and more formal restaurant upstairs. Authentic French cuisine complimented by one of the best wine lists in town with more than one hundred French vintages on offer, many of which are available by the glass. *Opening Times: Mon-Sat 5pm-12midnight*

L'ECRIVAIN `25 H8`
109a Lower Baggot Street, Dublin 2
Phone 661 1919
Price Rating: £££
Basement restaurant, serving classical French cuisine which makes great use of fresh, seasonal, Irish ingredients. Everything at L'Ecrivain runs smoothly as you would expect from one of the top restaurants in town. *Opening Times: Mon-Fri 12.30pm-2pm; Mon-Sat 6.30pm-11pm*

LEO BURDOCK'S `25 G8`
2 Werburgh Street, Dublin 8
Price Rating : £
There's no seating at Burdock's but it is worthy of a mention as it has been here since 1913 and serves arguably the best fish and chips in Ireland! The park down the road beside St Patrick's Cathedral is a good place to sit in judgement. *Opening Times: Mon-Fri 12.30pm-11pm; Sat 2pm-11pm*

LES FRERES JACQUES `25 G7`
74 Dame Street, Dublin 2
Phone 679 4555
Price Rating: £££
Situated across the road from Dublin Castle and next to the Olympia Theatre, Les Frères Jacques is one of Dublin's leading restaurants, serving *haute cuisine* in a setting which is unmistakably French. The menu takes advantage of a ready supply of fresh seafood, and the ambience is equally well suited to doing business or celebrating a special occasion. *Opening Times: Mon-Fri 12.30pm-2.30pm & 7.30pm-10.30pm; Sat 7.30pm-10.30pm*

LOBSTER POT `32 J9`
9 Ballsbridge Terrace, Dublin 4
Phone 668 0025
Price Rating: £££
Slightly old-fashioned restaurant which takes itself and

its customers rather seriously, but the food is top notch and includes a good choice of meat and poultry dishes as well as many fresh seafood options. *Opening Times: Mon-Fri 12.30pm-2.30pm; Mon-Sat 6.30pm-10.30pm*

LOCKS `31 G9`
1 Windsor Terrace, Portabello, Dublin 8
Phone 454 3391
Price Rating: £££
Nicely situated overlooking the Grand Canal, Locks is a serious but informal restaurant which pays great attention to detail, and all to good effect. The linen tablecloths and sparkling crystal set the tone for classical French cooking and an extensive wine list. Prices are on the expensive side, but then, there's no such thing as a free 'power lunch'. *Opening Times: Mon-Fri 12.30pm-2pm; Mon-Sat 7.15pm-11pm*

THE LORD EDWARD `25 G8`
23 Christchurch Place, Dublin 8
Phone 454 2420
Price Rating : £££
Located above a pub of the same name, just across the road from Christ Church Cathedral, the Lord Edward is Dublin's oldest seafood restaurant with a dining room in keeping with its period roots. The choice of fish is extensive and it comes cooked by whichever method you prefer. *Opening Times: Mon-Fri12.30pm-3pm; Mon-Sat 6pm-10.45pm .*

LUIGI MALONE'S `25 G7`
5-6 Cecilia St, Temple Bar
Phone 679 2723
Price Rating: ££
American in style, this large, split-level restaurant promises 'food from the four corners of the globe' which largely means pizzas, pastas, salads, burgers, steaks, and fajitas. All reasonably priced and served up in a very sociable atmosphere.

MAO `25 G8`
2-3 Chatham Row, Dublin 2
Phone 670 4899
Price Rating: ££
Very hip café bar serving oodles of noodles and much more besides. They describe it as Asian Fusion, which means that much of the food is quite hot and spicy, and so it might be wise to choose a cold Asian beer to help cool the taste buds. *Opening Times: Mon-Sun 9am-11.30pm*

MARRAKESH `25 G8`
28 South Anne Street, Dublin 2
Phone 679 4409
Price Rating: ££
There's a lot more to Moroccan cuisine than lamb and

couscous as you will discover in this upstairs restaurant, just off Grafton Street. *Opening Times: Tues-Sat 6pm-11.30pm*

MERMAID CAFE `25 G7`
69/70 Dame Street, Dublin 2. Phone 670 8236
Price Rating: ££
Hip and trendy hang-out serving innovative food complimented by a fine wine list. *Opening Times: Tues-Sat 12noon-3pm & 6.30pm-11pm*

MILANO `25 H8`
38 Dawson Street - phone 670 7744
19 East Essex Street - phone 670 3384 `25 G7`
Price Rating: ££
British chain, Pizza Express, prefer to operate in Dublin under the assumed name of Milano. What you get, however, is very much as you would expect - well chosen locations, designer interiors, pleasant service, a smart young crowd, and pizzas which are as good as you'll find anywhere in Dublin.

MONTY'S OF KATMANDU `25 G7`
28 Eustace Street, Temple Bar. Phone 670 4911
Price Rating: ££
Tandoori cooking, Nepalese style, in this cosy little restaurant in the heart of Temple Bar. Quentin Tarantino has eaten here, and they're proud of it, although Reservoir Dog has yet to make it onto the menu! The four course set lunch for £7.50 is great value. *Opening Times: Mon-Sun 12noon-3pm & 6pm-12midnight*

MOREL'S BISTRO `41 S14`
18 Glasthule Road, Dun Laoghaire
Phone 230 0210
Price Rating: ££
Stylish decor, mouth-watering bistro cuisine, excellent service and reasonable prices are just a few of the factors which help to keep Morel's so popular. *Opening Times: Mon-Sat 6pm-10pm; Sun 12.30pm-2.30pm & 6pm-10pm*

NICO'S `25 G7`
53 Dame Street, Dublin 2. Phone 677 3062
Price Rating : ££
Cosy but elegant restaurant which proudly claims to serve Italian cuisine in Irish style - a combination that clearly works judging by its popularity over the past thirty years. *Opening Times: Mon-Sat 12.30pm-2.30pm & 6pm-12midnight*

ODESSA LOUNGE & GRILL `25 G7`
13-14 Dame Court, Temple Bar
Phone 670 7634
Price Rating : ££
Fashionable restaurant which attracts quite a trendy

Kaffe Moka - a late night alternative to the taxi queue

crowd. The ground floor space is formally laid out for diners who choose from a menu with a rather cosmopolitan flavour, whereas downstairs is geared to the art of relaxation with lots of comfy sofas and low coffee tables. *Opening Times: Mon-Sun 12noon-12midnight.*

THE OLD DUBLIN `24 F8`
90-91 Francis Street, Dublin 8
Phone 454 2028
Price Rating : £££
Francis Street is renowned for its antique shops and the Old Dublin fits in well, with its open fireplaces and comfortable furnishings. The menu includes lots of fresh Irish fish but the cuisine comes all the way from Russia and Scandinavia. Look out for the special early evening menu which is available between 6pm and 7pm and costs only £10 per head. *Opening Times: Mon-Fri 12.30-2.30; Mon-Sat 6pm-11pm.*

OSUSHI! `25 G7`
12 Fownes Street, Temple Bar. Phone 677 6111
Price Rating: ££
Ireland's first Japanese sushi bar. Small but funky, serving authentic sashimi, temaki, and tempura. 8 pieces of sushi for one person costs £9; 32 pieces for four people costs £26. And no need to worry if you aren't too clever with chopsticks - most of what's on offer makes ideal finger food. *Opening Times: Mon-Sat 12noon-12midnight*

Eden - a place to see and be seen

PASTA FRESCA `25 G8`
2-4 Chatham Street
Phone 679 2402
Price Rating : ££
Despite the long opening hours, Pasta Fresca always seems to be bursting at the seams, but the staff are well drilled and they tend to cope with ease. Not surprisingly, fresh pasta dishes are the house speciality, and there's a good choice at very reasonable prices. And if you fancy a nice bit of something to take home, the deli counter will look after your needs. *Opening Times: Mon-Sat 8am-11.30pm; Sun 12.30-8.30pm*

PATRICK GUILBAUD `25 H8`
Merrion Hotel, Upper Merrion Street, Dublin 2
Phone 676 4192
Price Rating : £££+
This is the prize heavyweight (or coq of the walk!) of Dublin's French restaurants. The food takes advantage of a ready supply of fresh Irish ingredients, but the cooking is rigorously French and qualifies for a mention in all of the good food guides (Guilbaud's was the first restaurant in Ireland to be awarded two Michelin stars). Such a pedigree, however, comes at a price. Although there are some reasonably priced set menus, this is the land of expense account dining - so, if you intend paying by cash, be careful not to fall off your wallet when you sit down. *Opening Times: Tues-Sat 12.30pm-2.00 & 7.30pm-10.15pm*

PERIWINKLE SEAFOOD BAR `25 G8`
Powerscourt Townhouse, Clarendon Street
Phone 679 4203
Price Rating: £
One of several good eating places in the Powerscourt Townhouse, the Periwinkle enjoys very brisk trade by making extensive, but inexpensive, use of the day's local catch. Top of the pops is the seafood chowder. *Opening Times: Mon-Sat 11am-5pm*

RAJDOOT TANDOORI `25 G8`
26-28 Clarendon Street, Dublin 2
Phone 679 4274
Price Rating : ££
Situated behind the Westbury Hotel, the Rajdoot is one of Dublin's finest Indian restaurants. Tandoori cooking is the house speciality, but there are some interesting alternatives to chicken including several fish dishes and even quail! The menu is extensive and includes a good selection of vegetarian dishes, all served up in opulent surroundings. *Opening Times: Mon-Sun 1pm-2.30pm & 7.30pm-10pm*

ROLY'S BISTRO `32 J9`
7 Ballsbridge Terrace, Dublin 4
Phone 668 2611
Price Rating: ££
When it opened back in 1992, Roly's quickly became one of the most popular places in town. The fact that it has remained so owes much to the high standards of cooking and service, as well as a fashionable location close to the American embassy and RDS. The menu may change but the food is always beautifully prepared, keenly priced, and served up in a very relaxed atmosphere. *Opening Times: Mon-Sun 12noon-3pm & 6pm-10pm*

SENOR SASSI'S `31 H9`
146 Upper Leeson Street, Dublin 4
Phone 668 4544
Price Rating: ££
Conveniently situated if you are staying at the Burlington, Senor Sassi's has acquired a loyal following with its innovative cooking and sunny decor which both reflect a strong Mediterranean influence. *Opening Times: Mon-Fri 5.30pm-10.45pm; Sat 7pm-11.45pm; Sun 5.30pm-10.30pm*

SHALIMAR `25 G8`
17 South Great George's Street, Dublin 2
Phone 671 0738
Price Rating : ££
Excellent Punjabi cuisine served in tasteful surroundings which are reflected in the price. The Balti House downstairs offers an equally good, but slightly cheaper, alternative. *Opening Times: Mon-Sat 12noon-2.30; Mon-Sun 6pm-12midnight*

SINNERS `25 G7`
12 Parliament Street, Temple Bar
Phone 671 9345
Price Rating: ££
Cosy, Middle Eastern restaurant offering plenty of vegetarian options, and a range of mezzes if you prefer lots of variety.
Opening Times: Mon-Sun 6pm-late

SOUTH STREET PIZZERIA `25 G8`
South Great Georges Street, Dublin 2
Phone 475 2273
Price Rating: £
Trendy hang-out, serving good pizzas and pasta.
Opening Times: Mon-Sun 11am-1am

STEPS OF ROME `25 G8`
Chatham Street, Dublin 2
Phone 670 5630
Price Rating: £
Small diner staffed by Italians who know a thing or two about how to make a proper espresso, delicious pasta, and scrumptious pizza which comes by the slice. Seats are at a premium but prices are bargain basement.
Opening Times: Mon-Sat 10am-12midnight (until 1am Fri & Sat); Sun 1pm-10pm

TANTE ZOE'S `25 G7`
1 Crow Street, Temple Bar
Phone 679 4407
Price Rating: ££
Tasty Cajun-Creole cooking and an informal atmosphere which invites you to 'let the good times roll'.
Opening Times: Mon-Sun 12noon-4pm & 5pm-12midnight

THE TEA ROOMS `25 G7`
The Clarence Hotel, Wellington Quay, Dublin 2
Phone 670 9000
Price Rating: £££
Perhaps the coolest restaurant in town, and certainly a good choice if you are out to impress a prospective partner (in love, or in business for that matter). The modern cooking combines effortlessly with the elegant art deco surroundings. *Opening Times: Mon-Fri 12.30pm-2.30pm; Mon-Sun 6.30pm-10pm*

THUNDERROAD CAFE `25 G7`
Temple Bar, Dublin 2
Phone 679 4057
Price Rating: ££
Hard Rock Café meets Planet Hollywood meets TGI Friday. Get the idea? Big, brash, and American, a place where you are encouraged to let your hair down. The theme is Harley Davidson and custom motorcycles, while the food includes a range of burgers and a selection of creole/cajun dishes. *Opening Times: Sun-Wed 12noon-11.30pm; Thurs-Sat 12noon-12midnight*

TOSCA...NINI `25 G8`
20 Suffolk Street, Dublin 2
Phone 679 6744
Price Rating : ££
The folks back home may, or may not, be impressed to hear that you ate in a restaurant owned by Bono's broth-

Tosca - see the black board outside for the joke of the day

er, Norman, but Tosca is well worth a visit. The decor is simple but stylish, the food is mainly Italian and reasonably priced, and there's an innovative "Beat the Clock" policy operating between 5.30pm and 7pm Monday to Friday. The offer only applies to certain dishes, but you pay according to the time - order at 5.30pm and the dish costs £5.30. If you just fancy a decent cappuccino and a wide choice of some very good sandwiches, then pop next door to '....nini.' *Opening Times: Sun-Wed 11am-12midnight; Thurs-Sat 11am-1am*

TRASTEVERE `25 G7`
Temple Bar Square, Dublin 2
Phone 670 8343
Price Rating: ££
This stylish Italian eatery brings another dash of modernity to the historic Temple Bar district. Its glass walls provide a great vantage point to observe the hustle and bustle outside while enjoying a meal, or just a coffee, among the chic surroundings within. *Opening Times: Mon-Sun 12noon-11.30pm*

TROCADERO `25 G8`
3 St Andrew Street
Phone 677 5545
Price Rating: ££
One look at the richly decorated interior and the rogues gallery of luvvies that adorn the walls, and it should

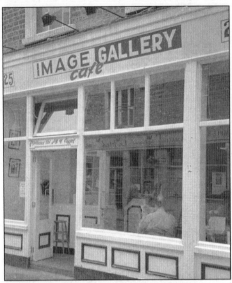

The Image Gallery - fine coffee & good photographs

ples! The style is informal, bordering on bohemian, the portions are generous, and the prices are cheap. Popular place, especially at lunchtime. *Opening Times: Mon-Sat 12noon-9pm*

THE WINDING STAIR `25 G7`
40 Lower Ormond Quay, Dublin 1
Phone 873 3292
Price Rating : £
The Winding Stair is one of Dublin's oldest bookshops, but it is also a quaint place to grab a bite of lunch as well as some good views of the River Liffey. An 18th century staircase connects the three floors, all of which are packed with books, and classical music plays in the background as the readers digest. *Opening Times: Mon-Sat 10.30am-6pm*

WRIGHT'S FISHERMAN'S WHARF `25 H7`
Financial Services Centre, Dublin 1
Phone 670 1900
Price Rating: ££
If you are seeking a change from the traditional face of Ireland, you have only to walk a few minutes from O'Connell Bridge to reach Dublin's financial quarter. Wright's enjoys an attractive setting, overlooking a dockland basin, surrounded by an array of modern architecture. Outside is reflected within, with an emphasis on modern design. The menu includes lots of seafood options, but more besides, and the cooking and presentation skillfully reflect the contemporary theme. *Opening Times: Mon-Fri 12noon-3pm; Wed-Sat 6pm-11pm*

come as no surprise to learn that the Trocadero enjoys a long and close association with nearby theatre land. The Italian food is simple and straightforward, but the secret of its enduring popularity has more to do with the fact that the Troc, above all, is a place to socialise, often long into the night when the show is over. *Opening Times: Mon-Sat 6pm-12.15am; Sun 6pm-11.15pm*

WAGAMAMA `25 G8`
South King Street, Dublin 2
Price Rating: ££
Part of a British chain of very hip noodle bars. The very successful formula is based on a designer cool interior where diners sit at long communal tables, and choose from an excellent range of reasonably priced rice and noodle dishes. Quirky touches include a hand-held, electronic device used by the waiting staff to record your food and drink orders and convey them, with the help of radio waves, to the open-plan kitchen.

WED WOSE `25 G8`
1b Exchequer Street, Dublin 2. Phone 670 8303
Price Rating: £
If you are looking for that last fry-up before your arteries finally fur up completely, go for the Builder's Breakfast and do your best to finish it before it finishes you!

WELL FED CAFE `25 G7`
6 Crow Street, Temple Bar. Phone 677 2234
Price Rating : £
A workers' co-operative dedicated to wholefood princi-

YAMAMORI `25 G8`
71-72 South Great George's Street
Phone 475 5001
Price Rating: ££
Yamamori equals stylish eating at low prices. The portions are generous and the Japanese cooking is full of flavour with plenty of choice for vegetarians. Noodles are the speciality of the house - they come stir-fried or in a soup, with a multitude of additional ingredients to add taste and texture. *Opening Times: Mon-Sat 12.30pm-2.30pm & 5.30pm-11pm; Sun 2pm-10pm*

ZEN `31 G10`
89 Upper Rathmines Road
Phone 497 9428
Price Rating: ££
Housed in a former Church of England meeting hall, owned by an Irishman but, thankfully, staffed by chefs specially brought over from China. The menu offers a wide choice of dishes from different regions of China, including some hot and spicy numbers from the Szechuan region. *Opening Times: Tues/Fri/Sun 12.30pm-2.30pm; Mon-Sun 6pm-12midnight*